AYSGARTH EDWARDIAN ROCK GARDEN

A STORY OF CREATION AND RE-CREATION

Aysgarth Edwardian Rock Garden

Aysgarth Edwardian Rock Garden was commissioned by Frank Sayer Graham in the early years of the twentieth century and is a rare surviving example of the work of the Backhouse firm of York. The garden is open to the public, free of charge, throughout the year. Contributions (via the donations box near the entrance) towards the upkeep and development of the garden are greatly appreciated.

The Rock Garden, 0.14 acres in size, was designed as a kind of "walk through grotto" with huge waterworn limestone blocks rising to about eight metres in places, low stone lintels and narrow winding paths. A cascade and stream-like rill add to the alpine atmosphere and at the rear of the garden the visitor emerges into an open south facing lawned area with mixed borders.

How to find Aysgarth Edwardian Rock Garden

Garden postcode: DL8 3AH, OS Grid reference: SE002883

If visiting by car please park in the lay-by and not directly outside the garden.

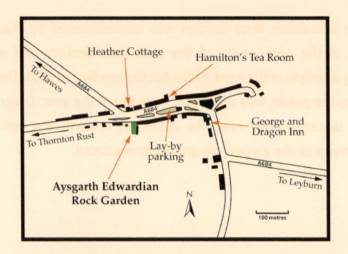

Please note that the garden is not suitable for disabled or wheelchair access due to narrow and uneven paths and steps. Visitors enter at their own risk and are requested to keep to the paths and to be aware of low stone lintels, open water and other potential hazards.

For further information about the garden or to contact the owners please visit: www.aysgarthrockgarden.co.uk

Rosemary Anderson's book *Aysgarth Edwardian Rock Garden - a Story of Creation and Re-creation* is now available from local retailers or via the website. It details the history of the garden and includes a descriptive guide to the planting accompanied by colour photographs.

AYSGARTH EDWARDIAN ROCK GARDEN

A STORY OF CREATION AND RE-CREATION

Rosemary Anderson

© Rosemary Anderson 2014

Published by Rosemary Anderson

All rights reserved. No part of this book may be reproduced, adapted, stored in a retrieval system or transmitted by any means, electronic, mechanical, photocopying, or otherwise without the prior written permission of the author.

The rights of Rosemary Anderson to be identified as the author of this work have been asserted in accordance with the Copyright, Designs and Patents Act 1988.

A CIP catalogue record for this book is available from the British Library.

ISBN 978-0-9928577-0-7

Book layout and cover design by Clare Brayshaw

Prepared and printed by:

York Publishing Services Ltd
64 Hallfield Road
Layerthorpe
York YO31 7ZQ

Tel: 01904 431213

Website: www.yps-publishing.co.uk

CONTENTS

	Foreword	vii
Chapter One	The Art Itself is Nature: The History of Rock Gardening	1
Chapter Two	A Well-Known Firm: James Backhouse and Son of York	8
Chapter Three	A Reputed Son: Frank Sayer Graham's Family	23
Chapter Four	A Private Rock Garden: The Story of Creation	33
Chapter Five	A Lifelong Resident of Aysgarth: Frank Sayer Graham	45
Chapter Six	A Quirky Wilderness: The Rock Garden in Decline	55
Chapter Seven	An Open Rock Garden: The Story of Re-creation	64
	Afterword	70
Appendix	The Rock Garden Today: A Descriptive Guide by A. Anderson	72
	References	91

ABOUT THE AUTHOR

Dr Rosemary Anderson specialised in historical geography during her undergraduate studies at The University of Sheffield in the 1970s, but she left the subject behind when she entered the teaching profession. During the years she was at home bringing up her family her interest in local history developed and in 1986 she published *Hayton 1762-1914: a Portrait of a North Nottinghamshire Country Parish*. In the 1990s Rosemary re-established her career within education and latterly worked as a specialist dyslexia teacher and researcher, completing her PhD in 2007. Since retiring and moving to Wensleydale she has spent much of her time learning about the area's fascinating past, and is currently Vice-Chair of the Middleham and Dales Local History Group. Rosemary and her alpine plant enthusiast husband, Adrian, became the owners of the Aysgarth Rock Garden in January 2012.

For up-to-date information about the Aysgarth Rock Garden please visit www.aysgarthrockgarden.co.uk

FOREWORD

In April 2005 an article in the Royal Horticultural Society (RHS) journal, *The Garden,* entitled "Uncovering a rocky past"[1] immediately drew my attention and that of my husband, Adrian. It told the story of the restoration of the Grade II Listed Edwardian Rock Garden at Aysgarth in Wensleydale, a rare surviving example of the work of the firm of James Backhouse and Son of York.[2]

The entrance to Aysgarth Rock Garden.

Although we thought we knew the area well, we were not aware of the garden's existence and so we resolved that the next time we travelled up to North Yorkshire from our home in Nottinghamshire we would visit. This we did soon afterwards and found ourselves amazed by the rockwork and charmed by the alpine planting. Little did we know then that we would move permanently to the area in the autumn of 2007 and that less than five years later, in January 2012, we would become the owners of the garden.

The Aysgarth Rock Garden was designed as a kind of "walk through grotto" with huge waterworn limestone blocks rising to about eight metres in places, low stone lintels and narrow winding paths. A cascade running down to a stream-like rill adds to the alpine atmosphere and at the rear of the garden the visitor emerges into an open south-facing lawned area with mixed borders.

This book reveals the history of the garden via two stories separated in time by around one hundred years – that of its creation in the early twentieth century by an Edwardian gentleman, Frank Sayer Graham of Heather Cottage, and that of its re-creation after restoration in the early twenty-first century by the then owners, Angela and Peter Jauneika.

Without Angela's vision there would be no Rock Garden today, and therefore no book. In view of this I acknowledge the enormous debt of gratitude I owe her and all those directly involved in the restoration project, as well as the many organisations and private individuals who contributed financially and in other ways to help ensure such a successful outcome. In addition, a great deal of information about the garden's history was researched by Angela in the years immediately prior to its restoration and generously passed on to me as an archive, and for that I also convey my heartfelt thanks for the time this has saved me.

Finally, I would like to draw attention to the dedication and hard work of my husband Adrian in maintaining the Rock Garden throughout the year. He has been a wonderful support in many ways during the process of producing this book and has contributed directly by taking all the photographs, unless otherwise stated. He has also written an appendix for the benefit of readers who have not visited the garden and this takes the form of an illustrated descriptive guide.

Dr Rosemary Anderson
West Witton, January 2014

CHAPTER ONE

THE ART ITSELF IS NATURE: THE HISTORY OF ROCK GARDENING

Introduction

> This is an art which does mend nature, change it rather, but THE ART ITSELF IS NATURE.

These words, taken from Shakespeare's *The Winter's Tale*, appeared at the start of an article entitled "A beautiful rock garden" in the horticultural journal *The Garden* of 12th June 1875.[3] Presumably the author, identified only by the initials H.N.H., chose to emphasise the final phrase in order to draw attention to its relevance to his/her subject, as there then followed a glowing description of a famous rockery whose artistry was considered to be on a par with the glories of the natural world. The appearance of this article and others like it must have fuelled interest in the emerging Victorian leisure activity of rock gardening, a passion that was to endure up to and beyond the end of the nineteenth century. In fact, as Nicola Shulman explains in her biography of alpine expert and plant hunter, Reginald Farrer:

> To the Edwardian eye, a limestone rockery planted up with alpine flowers would carry the refreshing connotation of a wild mountain landscape, and would confer . . . a cosmopolitan distinction upon its owner, as being one who visited the Alps in summer and saw these tiny beauties for himself.[4]

A view over the Rock Garden looking north.

It will never be known if this was the impression Frank Sayer Graham hoped to create when he decided he would like to have his own rock garden in Aysgarth, but in commissioning its construction he was definitely following a popular horticultural trend.

The origins of rock gardening

There is uncertainty amongst historians as to exactly how far back in time the origins of rock gardening can be traced,[5] and it is beyond the scope of this book to provide a detailed discussion of this subject. The well-known horticulturalist Graham Stuart Thomas wrote in 1989 of his belief that the development of rockeries sprang from the vogue for creating grottos as part of the "picturesque" landscape gardening movement of the mid to late eighteenth century.[6] Dark, damp, rocky grottos often had running water within them and so were ideal locations for ferns to grow, and this aroused people's curiosity about these plants. By the mid nineteenth century this interest had developed into a craze for collecting ferns in the wild, and then drying and pressing them. Graham Stuart Thomas went on to explain:

Group of dried and pressed British ferns (From F.G. Heath, *Garden Rockery*, 1908).

> Ferns in this country grow mostly in the woods, near streams and amongst rocks. Their collection took the seekers into just those places which were a delight to see and no doubt awakened many eyes to the beauty and savagery of rocky and mountainous scenery.[7]

The result was that, although the fern collecting hobby declined over time, the building of rockwork for the display of living specimens, known as ferneries, became popular and this interest within horticulture continued for many years. Even as late as 1908 Francis Heath devoted a substantial part of his book, *Garden Rockery: how to make, plant and manage it*, to the subject. In a chapter entitled "Fern rockery" he wrote a description of how he had constructed his own fernery, gave details of the main types of ferns available and even provided illustrations of pressed specimens.[8]

The firm of James Pulham and Son had developed a method in the 1820s of making artificial stone, called Pulhamite, which looked remarkably realistic when formed into rockwork because of the care taken to mimic geological formations and stratification.[9] The company became associated with the construction of ferneries for wealthy clients, and their ideas continued to exert influence as the vogue for creating what are now considered to be true alpine rock gardens began to take hold in the later nineteenth century.

Alpine plants become the focus

Androsace sarmentosa 'Chumbyi'
(from R. Malby, *The Story of my Rock Garden*, 1913).

As the international railway network developed, people began to travel more for leisure purposes and the well-off could afford to visit the Alps where they saw rocky scenery in abundance. Some were inspired to create their own miniature versions of the mountains, and initially the rockwork itself was considered to provide sufficient interest. However, delight was increasingly taken in having one's own collection of alpine flowers that had been seen in the wild, and although many species had been available from nurseries from the late eighteenth century onwards, on the whole they had been grown in separate sheltered beds away from the rockwork.

Gradually, the idea of making plants the focus and rocks the backdrop took hold as interest grew, fuelled by the exciting discoveries of intrepid plant hunters, who during this era went on expeditions to far flung parts of the world and brought back rare and unusual finds, either as seeds or live specimens.[10] The ability to successfully transport living plants by ship was transformed by the invention of the "Wardian case", a sealed protective glazed container that was the forerunner of the terrarium and which became widely used on long sea voyages from the mid nineteenth century onwards.[11]

Crocus versicolor **(from R. Malby, *The Story of my Rock Garden*, 1913).**

The influence of William Robinson

Books began to appear that were wholly devoted to the subject, one of the earliest being William Robinson's *Alpine Flowers for English Gardens*, which was published in 1870 after he travelled to the European Alps and Rocky Mountains of America to see plants in their natural surroundings. William Robinson went on to become a highly influential figure in the gardening world and in his foreword to the 1903 edition of the book, he made the important point that within horticulture the word "alpine" is used to denote plants that grow naturally within all high mountainous regions, not just the Alps.[12] He continued by extolling the virtues of alpine plants in a typically florid Victorian style:

> Above the cultivated land these flowers begin to occur on the fringes of the stately woods; they are seen in multitudes in the vast pastures which clothe many great mountain-chains, enamelling their soft verdure; and also where neither grass nor loose herbage can exist; or where feeble world-heat is quenched and mountains are crumbled into ghastly slopes of shattered rock by the contending forces of heat and cold, even there, amid the glaciers, they spring from Nature's ruined battle-ground, as if the mother of earth-life had sent up her loveliest children to plead with the spirits of destruction.[13]

Leontopodium alpinum – Edelweiss (from W. Robinson, *Alpine Flowers for Gardens*, 1903).

William Robinson was clearly passionate about his subject and as his stated aim was to show that alpines could be successfully grown in this country, by far the largest section of his book was given over to an A to Z gazetteer, which is generally accepted as the first detailed attempt to provide descriptions and advice on planting. His ambition was achieved, for by the end of the nineteenth century the cultivation of alpines had become such a popular horticultural pastime in the British Isles that a number of nurseries began to specialise in selling these plants. Some also became associated with the construction of rock gardens, the best known in the north of England being that of James Backhouse and Son of York. They were the firm who were commissioned by Frank Sayer Graham to build the Aysgarth Rock Garden, and in the next chapter I discuss their work extensively.

CHAPTER TWO

A WELL-KNOWN FIRM: JAMES BACKHOUSE AND SON OF YORK

The Backhouse firm in the nineteenth century

James Backhouse I,
1794-1869
(Rock Garden Archive).

The Backhouse family were Quakers, originally bankers from Darlington, but James Backhouse, born in 1794, became interested in botany after visiting Upper Teesdale and discovering rare alpine plants growing there in the unique arctic-like conditions.[14] When he was nineteen years old, James moved to Norwich to learn horticultural skills but in 1815 he came back to York and, along with his brother Thomas, bought the long established nursery firm of George Telford. This was conveniently situated in the centre of the city, but in 1830 George Hudson purchased the site in order to build York railway station and the firm moved across the river to Fishergate. In addition to his responsibilities with the family firm, James was a devout Quaker minister, and in 1831 he decided to leave his brother Thomas in charge of the nursery and travel to Australia as a missionary. During a ten year sojourn in various parts of the southern hemisphere he became enthralled with the flora and sent many new plants, including ferns, back to England for propagation at the Backhouse nursery in York and also at the Royal Botanic Gardens at Kew.

In 1841 James Backhouse returned home to his family in York. His 16 year old son, also called James, was developing an interest in botany and their shared passion meant that they started to explore upland areas of the British Isles together.[15] The younger James also became involved in the nursery business, and to avoid confusion, from now on the two Backhouse men will be referred to as James I and James II. After James I's brother Thomas died in 1845, the firm continued to thrive under the direction of father and son and in 1853 they moved to extensive new premises at Holgate on the western outskirts of York. Visitors were received at handsome offices near the entrance on Acomb Road, and the business, which was concerned with many types of horticulture in addition to alpines, was on such a huge scale that the total area of land covered by the nursery and show gardens extended to over one hundred acres.[16] Forty glasshouses were constructed and James II also built a magnificent gothic-style mansion, West Bank House, within the grounds, where, according to census records, he lived with his wife Mary, their two children, also called James and Mary, and a number of domestic servants.

James Backhouse II, 1825-1890 (Rock Garden Archive).

The rock garden at the York Nurseries

James I died in 1869, but in the capable hands of his son, James II, the firm came to occupy a pre-eminent position in its field in the north of England, and became sufficiently famous to be known simply as the "York Nurseries". A number of contemporary writers produced articles about the firm, and their aim seemed to be to show their readers how the nursery not only functioned as what would now be called a "garden centre" but also as a botanic garden and park. One feature in the grounds that attracted much interest was, unsurprisingly given the craze discussed in Chapter One, the underground glass-covered tropical fernery, but it was the two acre rock garden situated to the south of West Bank House that became the most famous. This was constructed during the late 1850s and was the particular creation of James II who wanted to show that alpine plants collected abroad could successfully be grown in this country. Built with sandstone brought from twenty or thirty miles away,[17] the rockwork rose to a height of almost ten metres in places and the design included ravines and even a small lake.

Surviving photographs of the Backhouse rock garden suggest that there was no attempt to make the rockwork look naturalistic with correct stratification. This was because, even though ardently interested in geology, James II believed that the most important outcome was to ensure that the correct microclimatic conditions were provided to suit the varying needs of the plants. Underpinning all his ideas was his highly developed scientific understanding, and this is revealed in the 1903 edition of William Robinson's book *Alpine Flowers for Gardens*, which included a section authored by James II before his death in 1890. In it he gave detailed instructions, illustrated with line drawn diagrams, on how to construct planting pockets in order to allow long root runs and, crucially, how to create fissures within the rockwork to ensure good drainage. In fact William Robinson held James II in such high esteem that he dedicated the 1903 version of his book to the memory of this late "mountain-lover, naturalist, and rock gardener".[18]

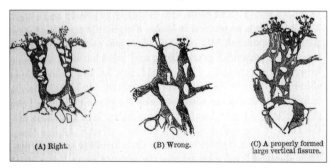

Diagrams on how to construct fissures by James Backhouse II (from W. Robinson, *Alpine Flowers for Gardens*, 1903).

The Backhouse rock garden (Rock Garden Archive).

The Backhouse rock garden no longer exists so it is hard to imagine its huge scale, but a visit in 2013 to the Royal Botanic Garden in Edinburgh has given me some idea of what the one at the York Nurseries might have looked like in its heyday. At Edinburgh an extensive rock garden was originally laid out in 1871 with a minimum amount of stone and numerous small straight-sided compartments for labelled plants. However, in 1914 it was remodelled using massive blocks of conglomerate and sandstone with no attempt at realistic stratification, and in that form, more in keeping with Backhouse design principles, it remains today.[19] The whole area, which contains around 5,000 plants, covers at least an acre and includes numerous winding paths and steps. These lead to a series of higher levels which provide vistas over a cascade, stream and large pond, the result being that overall the rock garden is an impressive sight for visitors.

The rock garden at the Royal Botanic Garden, Edinburgh.

Articles about the Backhouse rock garden

It is clear that the Backhouse show gardens were held in high regard in gardening circles from the mid nineteenth century onwards, and as early as 1864 the aforementioned William Robinson wrote about a visit to the York Nurseries in the influential journal *The Gardener's Chronicle*. In the extensive section in which he described what he called the "Alpine Rockery", he painted a vivid picture of its delights:

> The "rock-work" is best described as the facsimile of a very charming and well selected little bit of Wales or Cumberland, with its cliffs and ravine, little lake, rocky island, and gloomy gorge complete. It is utterly unlike and infinitely superior to any of the compositions known as "rock-work" that I have ever seen. Four hundred tons of "crag" rise in the most varied and rugged forms to 20-25 feet in height, surrounding and hemming in a placid sheet of water, and presenting every sort of nook, aspect, fissure, soil, shade, or shelter, that one could wish for the numerous and in many cases not easily to be pleased gems that flourish on the rock-work, from the water-overhanging slab, under which the Killarney fern looks at home, to the exposed ledge, where the alpine Forget-me-not thrives as if on its native Ben Lawers.[20]

As an aside, it would seem that William Robinson was particularly taken with what he later called the "cave" at the Backhouse rock garden for growing the delicate and rare *Trichomanes speciosum*, commonly known as the Killarney fern, as he included an illustration of it in the 1903 edition of his book.[21]

After providing the above general description of the Backhouse rock garden, William Robinson went on in his 1864 article to list hundreds of interesting and rare alpine plants that he found growing there, and finally wrote in conclusion:

> And so surprised and delighted to a degree previously unknown to me, I took leave of the York Nurseries . . . Often since I have concluded that were the famous "wishing carpet" at my service,

I should frequently during the coming spring and summer have a "rapid ride to York" and spend an hour amongst the delicately beautiful "transparencies of the tropical fernery", but for a real feast of interest I should settle down amidst the "heaven kissing" gems of the great Alpine Rockery there.[22]

The Backhouse cave for growing *Trichomanes speciosum* **– Killarney fern (from W. Robinson,** *Alpine Flowers for Gardens***, 1903).**

It perhaps comes as no surprise to reveal that the "beautiful rock garden" that inspired H.N.H. in 1875 to use the words quoted at the start of Chapter One was none other than the Backhouse one at the York Nurseries. This article described its subject in similar glowing terms to those used by William Robinson a decade earlier, but the author also included some useful details about the water management system by stating that "in parching weather, artificial showers from invisible fountains gently moisten the more exposed portions of the rockwork like a gentle rain".[23] An unpublished report resulting from a study during the 1990s to assess the feasibility of restoring the Backhouse rock garden confirmed the complexity of its nineteenth century hydraulic engineering by explaining that there were "many 'waterfalls' which were water piped to the top of rock formations, controlled by hidden taps and valves, thus acting as a simple irrigation system".[24]

The 1864 and 1875 articles quoted above were too early in date to have been read by Frank Sayer Graham, but another which may have caught his eye appeared in the *York Illustrated* magazine in 1894. This too was very complimentary about the Backhouse firm, and it is clear that their rock garden was still very impressive at that date as the author stated that the visitor:

Part of the Backhouse rock garden (from W.A. Clark, *Alpine Plants*, 1901).

> will discover that he is no longer amongst the plains or the mills of Yorkshire, but in a mimic Switzerland crowded with lake and mountain, crag and dell, and surrounded by the vegetation of Chamounix [*sic*] and guarded all round by Alpine firs and pines. This is not a fancy picture drawn for artistic effect; it is a truthful statement of the wonders contained in the York Nurseries.[25]

Backhouse trained gardeners

An article in the *Yorkshire Gardens Trust Newsletter* of Winter 2012 reminded readers of the often overlooked fact that "as well as being centres of horticultural skill and expertise, they [nineteenth century nurseries] were essential training grounds for gardeners".[26] This was certainly true of the Backhouse firm, which according to census records employed 109 men and 9 women in 1881. Their nationwide reputation ensured that some employees became famous in their specialist areas, one such person being Richard Potter, who was born in 1844. For many years supervisor of the rock garden at York, he was also involved in the construction of a number of rockeries for well-known clients throughout the British Isles.[27] The one that remains the most famous today, perhaps due to its association with former Beatle George Harrison, who bought the property in 1970, was that built for the renowned Victorian lawyer Sir Frank Crisp, at Friar Park, Henley-on-Thames.[28] Crisp, a passionate landscape gardener, acquired the house and estate in 1895, and soon afterwards decided to create an enormous alpine garden in the grounds. The Backhouse and Pulham firms were both involved with different portions of the rockwork, and the garden was so monumental in size that an unbelievable 23,000 tons of stone were used in its construction.[29] It included a lake, decorated underground caverns and, as a backdrop, a miniature version of the Matterhorn capped in shining quartz, using rock from the mountain itself. During its heyday this spectacular rock garden, which contained about 4,000 varieties of alpine plants, became very well-known as from time to time it was opened to the public for the benefit of charity.

Primula auricula marginata **(from W.A. Clark, *Alpine Plants*, 1901).**

Another Backhouse employee involved in the construction of the rock garden at Friar Park, who also became a renowned expert in his field, was William Angus Clark, born in 1856. He was listed in *Kelly's Directory of York* of 1905 as "Alpine Manager" for James Backhouse and Son, and lived at 20, The Mount, close to the York Nurseries. It has been possible to find out a good deal about William Angus

Clark's life because in 1901 he wrote a book entitled *Alpine Plants – A practical method for growing the rarer and more difficult alpine flowers*.[30] In the preface he described himself as having "long experience in the management of the very large collection of Alpine Plants cultivated in the York Nurseries",[31] and it would seem that he was also keen to showcase his connection with the Backhouse firm via the illustrations. A picture of part of the famous rockery was placed in a prominent position at the front, and there were also a number of close-up images of plants, some of which had been photographed at the York Nurseries. William Angus Clark was a Fellow of the RHS, which signified official recognition of his outstanding professional reputation, and unsurprisingly, given this accolade, he wrote in an authoritative style about the cultivation and choice of alpines for differing soil conditions.

The Backhouse firm in the early twentieth century

The firm of James Backhouse and Son still enjoyed a good reputation within horticultural circles at the end of the nineteenth and start of the twentieth centuries, but changes were taking place which meant that the role of the family was becoming less central. When the most inspirational of the Backhouse men, James II, died, aged 65, in 1890, the business was continued by his son, James III, and shortly afterwards became a limited liability company. James III, who was also an archaeologist and published ornithologist,[32] had married in 1890, and although at the time of the 1891 census he and his wife were still living at West Bank House with his widowed mother, sometime after that the couple moved away from York. By 1901 they were resident at Pannal, near Harrogate, where their household included four young children, two servants and two nurses. James III's occupation was given as "nursery and seedsman" and a contemporary advertisement reveals that the firm did have a branch in Harrogate in the late nineteenth century. However, a newspaper article of 1902 suggests that family involvement in the company was gradually diminishing. The report stated that a not-for-profit organisation, unique in this country at the time, to be known as the British Botanical Association, was to be formed to take over the scientific and educational department that had been established at the York Nurseries in 1900. Its remit was to supply specimens of plants for practical investigations by students and also to offer facilities for the agricultural trade to carry out "accurate seed testing and the investigation of plant diseases".[33] James III was named as one of the first directors, which shows that he retained involvement, but he was to share the role with three other men, two of whom had degrees in science.

Despite the changes, it would seem that around the time the Aysgarth Rock Garden was created, James Backhouse and Son continued to be held in high regard in alpine circles. The firm regularly won prizes for their miniature rockeries at the annual RHS Great Spring Show held at Inner Temple, London, the precursor of RHS Chelsea, and the famous rock garden at the York Nurseries also continued to be admired. Indeed, Edmund Jenkins, a contemporary authority, wrote in 1911 that:

[It is] probably the best example of its kind in a nursery garden in the country . . . Today it stands, as it has done for many a year in the past, as a monument to the good taste, ability, and perseverance of a former member of this well-known firm.[34]

Given the firm's pre-eminent reputation in the north of England, Frank Sayer Graham may well have travelled to the York Nurseries from time to time, but even if he did not actually visit, it is likely that he would have perused Backhouse alpine plant catalogues. These were beautifully illustrated and, in the words of the

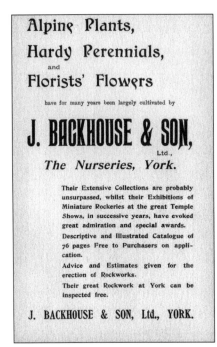

Advert for James Backhouse and Son Ltd (from W.A. Clark, *Alpine Plants*, 1901).

author of the *York Illustrated* article mentioned above, "of inestimable value both to the professional gardener, and the lady or gentleman amateur".[35] These words were perhaps inspired by the firm's stated aim, given in their 1898 catalogue, to provide readers with "a reference book and cultural guide, and not a mere tariff of prices".[36] Certainly when I inspected Backhouse catalogues of this era, held at the RHS Lindley Library, London, it was clear that that they provided a wealth of information on a huge range of alpines.

A note on Reginald Farrer

Perhaps because of his eccentric character and distinctive writing style, Reginald Farrer has become the best remembered of the Edwardian alpine enthusiasts and it has been speculated locally that he may have been involved in the creation of the Aysgarth Rock Garden. He lived at Ingleborough Hall, on the edge of the village of Clapham in the western part of the Yorkshire Dales, where he created his own rock garden in the grounds.[37] Very little remains but because he wrote at length about his preferred construction methods in his books, his strongly held views on the subject of rockwork are well known. In *The Rock Garden* of 1912

Saxifraga cochlearis **(from R. Farrer, *The Rock Garden*, 1912).**

he stated that only a small number of stones should be used and that they should be positioned horizontally in such a way as to give an appearance of natural stratification. To press his point further he included line drawings of how not to construct in order to show how dreadful what he called the "almond-pudding" and "plum-bun" rockery building systems appear to the eye.[38]

The almond-pudding building system (from R. Farrer, *The Rock Garden*, 1912).

The plum-bun building system (from R. Farrer, *The Rock Garden*, 1912).

Although Farrer openly acknowledged the influence of William Robinson on his interest in alpines, it is unlikely he would have shared the older man's delight in the rock garden at the York Nurseries. The following quotation shows how far Farrer's advice to would-be rock garden builders was from the Backhouse style of construction:

> Stone, in nature, is never disconnected; each block is always, as it were, a word in the sentence. Remember that, urgently: boulder leads to boulder in an ordered sequence. A dump of disconnected rocks, with discordant forms and angles, is mere gibberish. So you must take pains to treat your rocks as syllables: join them carefully up in harmonious order, and make your compilation a coherent whole.[39]

It is my belief that Farrer would have viewed the Aysgarth Rock Garden as a monstrosity, a view endorsed in 2013 by his biographer, Nicola Shulman, and it therefore seems unlikely he would have wanted to be associated with it. However, it is possible that Frank Sayer Graham travelled to Clapham from time to time to purchase alpine plants from the Craven Nursery, a commercial venture established by Farrer in the walled garden of Ingleborough Hall. Unfortunately the business did not prove to be a financial success, perhaps because as time went on his main focus of attention was on plant hunting in the Far East. This passion for adventure resulted in Farrer being away from home for much of the time from 1914 onwards and after falling ill on an expedition in 1920, he died in Upper Burma, aged only 40.[40]

Waterworn limestone at the Rock Garden.

The qualities of waterworn limestone

There was one topic on which Reginald Farrer was in agreement with most other gardening experts of his time, and that was with regard to the stone of choice for the rockwork. His preference was for the waterworn Carboniferous Great Scar limestone found in his native Craven district and further west, sometimes referred to as "Westmoreland", and the view that this stone is the best for rock garden construction has endured until the present day. Although the Carboniferous rock that forms the hard landscaping at Aysgarth is waterworn limestone, it is not the Great Scar type, but rather a darker grey-brown version that forms part of the sequence of Yoredale Beds. These are the narrow bands of alternating sandstone, shale and limestone that give the side slopes of Wensleydale their distinctive stepped appearance.[41] The qualities of the Yoredale limestone, however, are similar to that found in the Craven area and I end this chapter with Farrer's eloquent words:

> [Limestone] is far and away the best of all rockery formations. It is very helpful and nourishing to plants; and is also in itself, extraordinarily beautiful, waterworn into noble lines and crevices and irregularities.[42]

This description serves to draw attention back to the Asygarth Rock Garden, and in the next chapter I begin the story of its creation by looking at Frank Sayer Graham's family background.

CHAPTER THREE

A REPUTED SON: FRANK SAYER GRAHAM'S FAMILY

The western end of Aysgarth village showing the Rock Garden.

The Rock Garden plot

The plot of land in Aysgarth on which the Rock Garden stands has probably witnessed many centuries of human activity as field survey sites at the western end of the present village reveal a good deal of evidence of medieval occupation.[43] It is probable, given that the plot is in the middle of a line of roadside houses with crofts behind, that it was anciently the site of a cottage and small garth. However, it is unlikely this could ever be confirmed, because prior to the great rebuild in stone during the seventeenth century, most modest dwellings in the Yorkshire Dales were constructed mainly from wood, the result being that evidence rarely remains.[44] It would be fascinating to research the history of ownership of the plot back in time, but considerations of space and time preclude this, and so I start the story of the Rock Garden's creation in the mid nineteenth century when Aysgarth was a village of several hundred inhabitants, whose lives were firmly rooted in the agricultural economy of Wensleydale.

The tithe records

Many of the official government records generated in the years immediately after the Tithe Commutation Act of 1836 have survived, and due to their wealth of detail about ownership, occupation and land use, they provide information of direct relevance to the Rock Garden's history. The system of paying tithes in kind by giving a proportion of agricultural produce to the established church was essentially a medieval concept that was becoming increasingly difficult to operate from the late eighteenth century onwards. There was a general demand for commutation of tithes to a monetary payment, known as the "rent-charge", and although in some areas this had occurred during the process of enclosing common land, in many places the old system was still in place well into the nineteenth century. The Act of 1836 laid down the necessary procedures for a global amount of money to be agreed or compulsorily awarded for each community, and this sum then had to be apportioned between all the landowners as fairly as possible. Although not ideal, as the state of cultivation of the land could change over time, the only practicable way to do this was to gather accurate details of acreage and land use. A surveyor was therefore commissioned to conduct a survey and draw up a plan at a large scale, now often referred to as the "tithe map", and then an accompanying schedule detailing each owner's individual rent-charge was prepared, usually by a professional valuer.[45]

Francis Sayer, yeoman farmer

In Aysgarth the old system of paying tithes in kind was still largely in place prior to the 1836 Act and so the landholders held a meeting on 9th October 1840 in order to determine the global amount of money to be paid. However, it would seem they were unable to reach agreement on the issue because the total rent-charge was compulsorily awarded on 31st December 1841.[46] The land survey and apportionment then went ahead, and the tithe map, which has survived in good condition, along with the accompanying written documentation, was published in 1843.[47] A professional land surveyor, William Alderson of Leyburn, drew up the map, but the tithe records for Aysgarth reveal a somewhat unusual situation because five local men acted as valuers. One of them was Francis Sayer, a person of significance in this story because he is named in the written schedule as the owner of the Rock Garden plot. This can be seen on the map marked as open ground and divided into two parts by some sort of boundary. The tithe details also show that Francis owned and occupied the house and yard across the road, now known in extended form as Heather Cottage. The land use description for the Rock Garden plot states that it was classified as garden and that the state of cultivation was "arable". This most probably means that it was used to grow vegetables for the house, as the plots which now form the garden and grounds of Heather Cottage were not then owned by Francis.

St Andrew's Church, Aysgarth (from H. Speight, *Romantic Richmondshire***, 1897).**

Postcard of Heather Cottage and Aysgarth before the Rock Garden was built (Rock Garden Archive).

The tithe records also show that Francis Sayer owned about five acres of meadow, formerly common land, alongside the road to Thornton Rust, which was tenanted out, and that he rented a further seventy acres, mainly classified as meadow or pasture. It is probable that Francis also owned some land in other parts of Wensleydale, as in his will of 1871 he described himself as a "yeoman".[48] This term survived until the early twentieth century in some rural areas to denote farmers who were relatively wealthy, but could not be considered to be of the gentry class. Although Francis was a modest landowner, as one of the tithe valuers, it would seem likely that he was of a social standing that commanded considerable respect within the community.

The census records

Further information about Francis Sayer can be found in the census returns, another invaluable set of historical records that exist from the mid nineteenth century onwards, and which have already been referred to in Chapter Two in relation to the Backhouse family. The ten-yearly

Census of England and Wales began in 1801 but the first four were a head count only, and it was not until 1841, when the census became the responsibility of the Registrar General, that much more detailed information was collected. Locally appointed enumerators gave the head of each household a schedule to be filled in and on this they were required to provide details of all the persons resident on the chosen Sunday night, even if only temporary visitors. The forms were collected the following day and the information was then copied into enumerators' books which are currently available for the censuses up to and including 1911.[49]

The 1841 census records for Aysgarth list Francis Sayer as the head of his household and give his age as 45, but at that date the ages of adults were rounded down, and he was in fact several years older. The details also reveal that he was born in Yorkshire, was living with two elderly persons and a young female servant, and was working as a "cattle dealer". Marie Hartley and Joan Ingilby relate in *Life and Tradition in the Yorkshire Dales* that such trading of cattle, sometimes acquired locally, but often brought down by drovers from Scotland to be sold on at Dales markets, had long been a way of making a living in the local area.[50]

In the 1851 census records for Aysgarth, when fuller details of individuals are given and ages are accurately shown, Francis Sayer appears again as the head of a household, age 59, born in Coverdale, and now described as a "farmer of 16 acres". His marital status is given as single and his household at that date consisted of himself and an unmarried female "house servant", Elizabeth Graham, who had been born in the nearby village of West Witton, famous for its Feast and the ancient ceremony of "Burning owd Bartle".[51]

Frank Sayer Graham's early life

In 1861 Francis Sayer, now aged 69, continued to make his living as a farmer "of 55 acres". He was still single, but the census records show that he had promoted his servant Elizabeth Graham, who was 36 and still unmarried, to the role of "housekeeper". It is at this point that the details become directly relevant to this story. Included in the 1861 listing is a boy, aged one year, who is described as the son of the head of the household, and is named as Francis Graham. This baby was the person who in adult life would commission the construction of the Rock Garden and his birth certificate shows that he was born to Elizabeth on 21st June 1859 in West Witton, where, according to the 1861 census, members of her family still lived. The baby was officially registered on 8th July as "Francis Sayer Graham" by his mother, who made her mark because she was unable to sign her name, and it is here that a mystery is revealed regarding paternity. Despite giving the child the middle name "Sayer", the sections on the form for the father's name and occupation are left blank. Similarly, the parish register for West Witton shows that the baby was baptised as "Francis Sair [*sic*] Graham" at the village church on 24th August, but again no father is named even though the details were not annotated with the word "illegitimate" as some entries were around that date.

Village scene, West Witton (from E. Bogg, *Beautiful Wensleydale*, 1925).

Deepening the uncertainty is the fact that the child is repeatedly referred to as his "son or reputed son" by Francis Sayer in his will of 1871, mentioned earlier in this chapter. Enquiries as to the meaning of the word "reputed" in historical sources suggest that it could be used to signify a child generally regarded as a son or daughter, but who was not so in biological terms. In the light of commonly held views of strict Victorian morals it is surprising to discover an elderly unmarried man of some standing in the community living with a middle-aged woman, socially his inferior, together with a child openly acknowledged as his son. Perhaps it is time to revise the somewhat stereotypical view of how unconventional domestic arrangements were regarded in the nineteenth century. What is most important is to acknowledge that Francis senior obviously decided to stand by Elizabeth and regard her son as his own, and to avoid confusion, from now on the boy, Francis junior, will be referred to as Frank, the name he was known by locally and by his family throughout his adult life.

The family in the late nineteenth century

The census records of 1871 reveal that the details of the household remained the same as in 1861 except that Frank, now 11 years old, is listed as a "scholar". However, a big change was soon to take place within the family as Francis died on 17th December 1871, aged 80, and was buried in Aysgarth churchyard. Unusually, a detailed map and schedule of property and land ownership and occupation, drawn up in a similar format to the earlier tithe records and prepared as part of the Aysgarth Union Valuation of 1872, exists within the records of the now defunct Aysgarth Rural District Council.[52] This document provides much additional relevant information at a date just after Francis died because individual plots of land are numbered in exactly the same way as on the 1843 tithe map. The records show that the Aysgarth estate of Francis Sayer was then in the hands of his devisees and reveal that in addition to the five acres of land he owned in 1843, he had in the intervening years acquired around twenty additional acres of grassland, currently rented out, all at the western end of the village. The two sections of what is now the Rock Garden were still used as before to grow vegetables, and he had bought the small plot of land behind the house and yard to provide more garden. Elizabeth Graham is shown as the occupier of the house and gardens, and Francis' will of 1871 confirms that he regarded her and his "reputed son" Frank as his dependents because he made provision for them after his death by leaving his house and a small paddock nearby in trust for their use. He also bequeathed his "household furniture and effects" including "dairy and farming utensils" to them, so it would seem that he expected them to continue with an agricultural way of life. Although he also left annuities to two relatives, it is clear that Francis saw Elizabeth and Frank as the rightful inheritors of the majority of his estate. Vitally, in those days prior to the welfare state, he ensured Elizabeth's financial security via a yearly sum of money, provided that she did not marry, and Frank's via an inheritance to be paid to him at age 21.

In the 1881 census returns, Elizabeth appears as a single lady aged 56, the head of her household, and as expected, classed as an "annuitant". Living with her is her unmarried son, now aged 21, described as an "unemployed clerk" and significantly named as "Francis S". Perhaps on reaching the age of majority on 21st June 1880 and receiving his inheritance, Frank decided to start to use his middle name in order to keep alive the memory of his father, something he did for the rest of his life.

By the time of the 1891 census, Frank, now aged 31, had become the head of his household, and the details reveal that his financial situation had become comfortable. He was now described as "living on own means" and was wealthy enough to employ a 15 year old live-in domestic servant. Individual addresses are rarely given for modest rural properties in census enumerators' books, but it would seem that he was living in his father's house as *Bulmer's Directory of the North Riding* of 1890 listed Francis Sayer Graham of Heather Cottage, Aysgarth. The 1891 census also reveals that an important domestic change had taken place as Frank now had a 24 year old wife, Mary Elizabeth, who had been born in Llangurig, mid-Wales. According to the couple's marriage certificate, she was the daughter of William Jones, a farmer, and the wedding was solemnised on 31st December 1885 at the parish church of Huntley in Gloucestershire. It is interesting to note that Frank gave his occupation as "farmer" on the form, thereby providing the only documentary evidence I have found where he is recorded as being of that occupation. It is also revealing, given the above discussion, that the columns for the bridegroom's father's name and occupation are left blank, which suggests that Frank was aware of the uncertainty over the paternal status of Francis Sayer. Frank's mother, Elizabeth Graham, was still alive in 1891, and is recorded in the census as living alone "on own means" at a different unspecified address in the village. She died in August 1892, aged 68, and was buried with Francis Sayer in Aysgarth churchyard.

The family in the early twentieth century

The 1901 census records show that Frank and his wife Mary had no children and reveal that at that date he was earning his living as a "game dealer" based at home and working on his "own account" – in other words, self-employed. It would seem he was doing well because they now had sufficient income for the household to include two female servants, one described as a "housemaid" and the other as a "general servant". Moving on in time to 1911, Heather Cottage is finally given as the couple's address and extra information sought by the census that year showed that they had now been married for twenty-five years and still had no children.

Lady Hill, Wensleydale.

Although Frank did trade in game birds, it is via his involvement in selling silver-grey rabbits for their fur that his name has remained famous as a dealer in the local area. A large commercial warren of seventy-five acres, originally belonging to the Metcalfes of Nappa Hall, had long existed at Woodhall, a little further west along Wensleydale, where its highest part, Lady Hill, is visible from the Rock Garden.[53] The sought-after rabbits bred at the warren were larger than wild rabbits and were particularly prized for their close black fur with white hairs that shone like silver in the sun. During the late nineteenth century the warren was owned by the Vyners of Newby Hall, and in their book, *A Dales Heritage*, Marie Hartley and Joan Ingilby relate details via the diaries of Harry Storey, the gamekeeper who acted as warrener from 1894 to 1922. They describe how:

> Many [rabbits], mostly alive, were bought by the game dealer F.S. Graham of Aysgarth for 2s. each. Some went to stock burrows in other parts of the country and a few went to America. The fur became fashionable as a lining for tweed motor coats, and King Edward VII sent one of these handsome garments to the Tsar of Russia, Nicholas II. [54]

It is not known how much money Frank inherited from his father or if he had other sources of income, but clearly the trade in rabbit fur was of high status, so it may have been this line of business that enabled him to be in a financial position to commission the Rock Garden, and in the next chapter I tell the story of its creation

CHAPTER FOUR

A PRIVATE ROCK GARDEN: THE STORY OF CREATION

The commissioning of the Rock Garden

It is tempting to speculate that Frank Sayer Graham may have been inspired to create the Rock Garden because he was an admirer of Thomas Bradley's "admirable Alpine garden, abounding in choice botanical rarities" which was situated at Bear Park, near Aysgarth Falls.[55] According to Harry Speight, who wrote the above description in his 1897 book *Romantic Richmondshire*, this garden had recently been developed and he considered it of sufficient interest to merit the inclusion of a photograph. Bear Park is a substantial stone built farmhouse on the north bank of the River Ure which dates back to the seventeenth century and has many interesting architectural features.[56] Census records of the late nineteenth and early twentieth centuries reveal the intriguing detail that Thomas Bradley, the unmarried yeoman farmer who owned the property, had been born in New York in 1835 but was classified as a

The alpine garden, Bear Park (from H. Speight, *Romantic Richmondshire***, 1897).**

British citizen. He was somewhat older than Frank, but would seem to have been of a similar social standing and so it is possible that the two men may have known each other and spent time together, given their mutual interest in alpine plants.

Once Frank had made up his mind to create a rock garden it is not surprising, given their pre-eminent reputation in the north of England, that he commissioned James Backhouse and Son of York to build it. A section at the end of one of the firm's plant catalogues from around the time the Rock Garden was constructed gives a fascinating insight into their working practices and shows that their marketing skills were well developed:

> The Landscape Department is directed by a thoroughly experienced expert designer, assisted by a competent staff. In practice we find it advisable and a saving of cost, to first view the site, and ascertain the wishes of the owner with regard to treatment; afterwards to draw out and submit a plan for approval.
>
> Skilled foremen, with thorough knowledge of Garden making, are placed in charge of the work, with capable assistants if the size of the contract necessitates it. Other labour is usually obtained locally to minimise the cost.
>
> A selection [of plants] can always be made from OUR OWN large, healthy stocks and thus materially lower the cost. In the case of Rock Formations the necessary plants are cultivated in our own Alpine grounds at York.[57]

The reasons why Frank decided to use the plot opposite Heather Cottage for the Rock Garden rather than the land purchased by his father at the rear of the house, with its direct access from the yard, will never be known. It has been suggested locally that he chose the prominent position next to the road so that he could signal his status and wealth to all. By the early twentieth century, the Falls on the River Ure, less than a mile away, were already a popular tourist destination and so many visitors in addition to local people would pass through Aysgarth village and potentially be able to marvel at his evocation of the Alps in miniature.

It is possible, however, that the decision on siting may have simply been one of practicality linked to advice from Backhouse experts after a site visit. The chosen plot does conform fairly closely to the first four of five rules for making a rock garden laid out in articles in *The Garden* magazine in 1923, admittedly a somewhat later date:

> It must be in the open, unshaded by trees; it should run from north to south, so as to ensure westerly or easterly exposure; there should be a difference in level between one end and the other; this fall in level should again be on the north-south axis; and there should be "a solid background of trees or shrubs at the northern end".[58]

Certainly the shape of the plot with its gradual rise from north to south leant itself readily to the design of a "walk through grotto", and the situation chosen for the Rock Garden also made it ideal for viewing from the principal rooms of Heather Cottage.

The Rock Garden must have taken a considerable time to construct given the complexity and scale of the rockwork, and according to the wording of the Grade II Listing it was built between 1906 and 1914. However, it seems unlikely it would have been in the making for as long as eight years and as no original administrative documentation has ever come to light I would suggest that these dates are an approximate "best guess" made by English Heritage experts in 1988. It is frustrating not to be able to be more exact on this matter, but fortunately it is possible to be certain as to who was in charge of the works. That person was William Angus Clark, the Backhouse Alpine Manager and author of *Alpine Plants*, mentioned in Chapter Two, and the reason this information is known will be explained below. In his writing he always referred to himself as "Mr Clark", and so from now on that form of his name will be used.

The second edition of *Alpine Plants* and Mr Clark's involvement

**The rock garden at The Pleasaunce
(from W.A. Clark, *Alpine Plants*, 1907).**

The 1901 edition of Mr Clark's book must have been well received because in 1907 a second, enlarged and fully revised, version appeared, with the somewhat altered title, *Alpine Plants – A practical manual for their culture*.[59] Perhaps this suggests that on reflection the inclusion of the phrase "*more difficult alpine flowers*" in the 1901 title was felt to be off-putting for potential purchasers. The photograph at the front was also changed to one of the extensive rock garden at The Pleasaunce, Overstrand, Cromer, showing an ornamental lake in the foreground in the then fashionable Japanese style. This rock garden had been constructed by Mr Clark to a design by the wealthy owner, Lord Battersea, and an article about it appeared in *The Yorkshire Herald* in February 1907. The anonymous author provided a review of the new edition of *Alpine Plants* at the start of the article which was full of praise for Mr Clark and described him as being "well known as an expert in Alpine plant culture and in the construction of artistic rockeries and Alpine gardens".[60] Indeed, his fame was such that the author went on to say that "Her Majesty the Queen

[Alexandra], who visited the Pleasaunce last year, was . . . delighted with its beauty, and she graciously expressed her willingness to receive a copy of Mr Clark's book, when the second edition should be ready".[61]

Another difference between the two editions of *Alpine Plants* was that in the 1907 version Mr Clark inserted a frontispiece in which he listed seventeen "places where work has been carried out under his planning and supervision".[62] Many of the rock gardens were on a large scale such as The Pleasaunce, mentioned above, and Friar Park, described in Chapter Two, but some on the list were of more modest proportions, a local example being at Neville Hall, Middleham, for "H. Maughan Esq.", who according to the 1901 census was a middle-aged solicitor. However, because of its vital importance to this story, the name that stands out is that of "F.S. Graham Esq., Heather Cottage, Aysgarth". The inclusion of the Rock Garden on the list means it can be said with certainty that Mr Clark was in charge of the works and also proves that it must have been in existence in some form by the start of 1907.

By kind permission of the Owners specified, Mr. Clark is enabled to cite the following places where work has been carried out under his planning and supervision, as examples from among many others :—

Lady Ardilaun, St. Anne's, Dublin.
The Right Hon. Lord Battersea, Overstrand, Cromer.
Mrs. H. W. Jefferson, Stoke Rochford Hall, Grantham.
Mrs. A. Wilson, Tranby Croft, Hull.
Rev. C. A. Barry, Clifford, Boston Spa.
C. Blackett, Esq., Toulston Grange, Tadcaster.
F. Crisp, Esq., Friar Park, Henley-on-Thames.
F. Green, Esq., Treasurer's House, York.
G. Goodrick, Esq., The Close, Knaresbro'.
F. S. Graham, Esq., Heather Cottage, Aysgarth.
W. N. Hicking, Esq., Brackenhurst Hall, Notts.
C. D. Leng, Esq., Sandy Gate, Sheffield.
H. Maughan, Esq., Neville Hall, Middleham.
G. Marchette, Esq., Manor Heath, Halifax.
J. Ogston, Esq., Kildrumney Castle, Aberdeenshire.
G. S. Thompson, Esq., Newbuilding, Thirsk.
Rev. W. Travis, Ripley, Yorks.

Frontispiece list of gardens worked on by Mr Clark (from W.A. Clark, *Alpine Plants*, 1907).

Amazingly, a second piece of dating evidence came to light at the time of restoration in 2002-3 when a postcard of Aysgarth, showing a view of Heather Cottage and the roadside prior to the existence of the Rock Garden, was bought by a local collector. She realised that the message on the back provided crucial information because it was written in a boyish hand by Mr Clark's son Tom, who, census records reveal, would have been about 9 years old at the time. The postcard

37

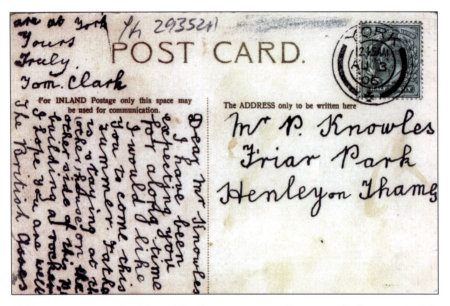

Message written by Tom Clark on reverse of postcard, August 1906 (Rock Garden Archive).

was addressed, tellingly, to a Mr Knowles at Friar Park, Henley-on-Thames, and was postmarked York, August 3rd 1906, the relevant part reading "Father is staying at the (other) house on the other side of this PC building a rockery".[63] This postcard therefore not only confirms a year when construction was definitely taking place, but also pinpoints a specific month when Mr Clark was actively in charge. Local knowledge has added to the details known about him as it is said that he earned £1 a day, always wore gloves, carried a type of crowbar known locally as a gavelock, and only went back to his home in York every third week. This suggests that he was a conscientious and dedicated supervisor of the works and it seems likely he was highly experienced in the construction side of rock gardening, for his creation has remained in a largely structurally sound condition for over one hundred years.

The construction of the Rock Garden

It is likely that Frank's means were relatively modest compared to many of the people for whom Mr Clark worked, and this, taken alongside the

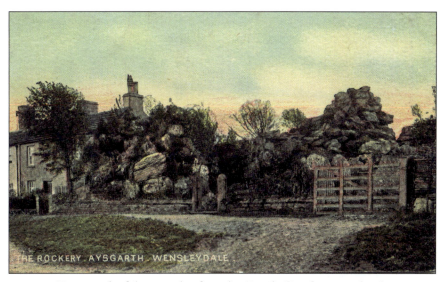

Postcard of Aysgarth after the Rock Garden was built (Rock Garden Archive).

difficulty and expense of transporting heavy materials prior to the age of motor transport, must have meant it was only feasible to build the Rock Garden if there was suitable stone nearby. A long-term resident of Aysgarth who remembers Frank has said that he was very good at seizing his chance for procurement in the vicinity, and that the boulders were brought from an area known as Stephen's Moor, near Seata Quarry, only about half a mile west towards the village of Thornton Rust. Significantly, the current 1:25,000 Ordnance Survey map marks a portion of this land as "quarry – disused" and also reveals the presence of old lead mine workings and shafts in the vicinity. The result of this past disturbance is that Stephen's Moor is now an undulating area of rough grassland dotted with ancient hawthorn trees, but here and there large stones can be seen bearing considerable similarity to those forming the Rock Garden. It is hard to know what this area would have looked like before the rock was extricated in an act that today would be considered a totally unacceptable form of environmental vandalism. It is possible that the limestone lay exposed on the surface, but more likely it was overlain by a thin layer of soil and grass as at present, its waterworn appearance being the result of erosion by the many small and intermittent streams that emerge from springs and run down the hillside. Although most of the Rock Garden stone came from Stephen's Moor, it has been said that the material used to form the largely unseen core was taken from the bed of the River Ure when a footbridge replaced stepping stones just west of Aysgarth, and certainly one water-pitted boulder close to the stream looks markedly different from those nearby.

It must have been a huge task to extract the hundreds of tons of rock, and local knowledge suggests that the labouring work was done by employees from Burtersett Quarry, further up Wensleydale near Hawes.

Stephen's Moor, near Aysgarth.

Apparently a "stone waggon", a long narrow low-slung cart with four wheels, provided by the quarry, was used to transport the boulders the short distance to the garth adjacent to the Rock Garden where it was unloaded by crane. Once alongside the plot some sort of mechanical means would have been needed to manoeuvre the stone into place, but unfortunately I have not been able to discover any details. However, in

The Garden article of 1875, referred to in Chapters One and Two, H.N.H. does confirm that, in relation to the construction of the rockery at the York Nurseries, the Backhouse firm had "rough but effective machinery for lifting them [i.e. the stones] respectively into their final positions",[64] and something similar must have been used at Aysgarth. What is certain is that even if eight years seems an unfeasibly long time, the process of building the Rock Garden must have been a slow and arduous job for the labourers involved. No original documents detailing the actual method of construction survive, but a structural survey completed before restoration in 2002 usefully explains that most of the rocks are:

> laid on a dry bed, interlocking one on top of the other, however in places there is evidence of the use of lime mortar cementing in smaller stones and packing out crevices. The boulders stacked up on top of each other create a number of high rocky outcrops . . . In general these outcrops are formed by placing stone upon stone, tapering towards the top. However, the exceptions to this typical arrangement are individual stones cantilevering out from this line, one overhanging rock face, and a recessed area supported with two columns.[65]

The Rock Garden Archive contains a photocopy of a *Schedule of prizes, rules and regulations of Aysgarth and District Floral and Industrial Society*, prepared for the second annual show to be held on 18th August 1909. It is tempting to wonder if Mr Clark might still have been involved in the creation of the Rock Garden at this date as he is recorded as providing a number of prizes. These were in the form of climbers, flowering shrubs, roses and pyramid fruit trees, and although some were for individual horticultural classes, one was especially prestigious as it was for the overall winner of the two main sections. It is possible that Mr Clark had given advice on the setting up of the show in the preceding years, because around this time he was a Vice-President of The Ancient Society of York Florists, the oldest horticultural society in the world.[66] According to local knowledge the Aysgarth show was always held at Bear Park and Thomas Bradley, mentioned at the start of this chapter, is named in the schedule as a Vice-President of the local Society. Perhaps surprisingly there is no mention of Frank Sayer Graham in the list of officials and subscribers and it will never be known if he submitted entries to the show as no results have come to light. Given his passion for gardening it seems likely that he would have taken part, especially as he retained the rear open area of the Rock Garden for growing vegetables, in an echo of the plot's nineteenth century usage.

The planting of the Rock Garden

Ramonda pyrenaica (from R. Malby, *The Story of my Rock Garden*, 1913).

Eventually the hard landscaping of the Rock Garden must have been completed to Mr Clark's satisfaction in the style advocated by James Backhouse II, mentioned in Chapter Two, so that a variety of microclimates to accommodate the differing needs of alpine plants were provided and good drainage ensured through fissures in the rocks. The job of importing soil to create planting pockets in the ledges and crevices of the stones, both in sunny and shady aspects, would have then taken place before the final task of planting up with choice specimens of alpines went ahead. It is likely that these were purchased from the Backhouse firm, as the quotation from their catalogue at the start of this chapter gives the impression that they could be obtained at a discount, although it is possible that some were propagated at home by Frank himself.

Remarkably, a few of the original plants are thought to have survived to the present day, a particularly noteworthy example being a *Ramonda pyrenaica* on a north facing ledge near the entrance to the garden.

According to the 1911 Backhouse catalogue this "plants a rosette of leaves against the shaded side of rocks and makes an admirable picture when full of blue, gold centred bloom".⁶⁷ This plant was viewed at the Backhouse rockery and picked out for special mention by H.N.H. as early as 1875 in *The Garden* article referred to in Chapters One and Two. It must have continued to have been considered of particular merit as it appears in a black and white photograph in the 1901 version of Mr Clark's *Alpine Plants* and also as an exquisitely coloured plate at the front of the 1913 edition of Reginald Malby's, *The Story of my Rock Garden*.⁶⁸

Asplenium scolopendrium – **hart's tongue fern growing in the Rock Garden.**

Alpines would not have been the only type of plants chosen for the garden at the time of its creation. Ferns were still fashionable and a number of examples of *Asplenium scolopendrium*, commonly called the hart's tongue fern, which may be descendants of original specimens, are still present. There is also a bamboo, situated on the edge of the lawned area at the rear, evidence of the interest in Japanese style planting at the time of the creation of the garden, and another of Mr Clark's specialities, according to the frontispiece of the 1907 edition of his book. He was also probably responsible for the engineering of a cascade that ran down to the stream-like rill as he also listed water gardens as an area of expertise. According to local knowledge, this water feature was fed by a now non-existent spring on the hillside above the garden, and worked via gravity using lead pipes and a header tank at the rear of the garden.

Frank's Private Rock Garden

Sign on the entrance gate to the Rock Garden.

Maybe the final tasks associated with the construction of the Rock Garden were the building of the stone boundary walls on three sides, and the erection of the iron railings and gate adjacent to the road on the fourth side. An original rectangular sign on the gate reads "PRIVATE ROCK GARDEN" and this was very much how Frank wished it to remain. Entry was definitely by invitation and only for adults and it would seem this rule was strictly enforced. According to a long-term resident of Aysgarth, Frank's second wife would rap on the windows of Heather Cottage if she noticed children even as much as approaching the railings across the road. Perhaps they could be forgiven for looking in as the tantalising glimpses from the entrance must have revealed the Rock Garden as potentially a most appealing adventure playground. However the garden was not totally private even in Frank's day. His last maid, Doris Levill, who worked at Heather Cottage from 1936 to 1946, related at the reopening of the garden after restoration in 2003 that if Frank saw tourists or hikers looking from the road, he would show them round in return for a donation to his favourite "waifs and strays" charity. Frank was clearly a public spirited man who had many interests in addition to his passion for horticulture, and in the next chapter I look more closely at his life in Aysgarth.

CHAPTER FIVE

A LIFELONG RESIDENT OF AYSGARTH: FRANK SAYER GRAHAM

Heather Cottage showing the Arts and Crafts extension.

Frank and his first wife, Mary

Around the same time that the Aysgarth Rock Garden was created, Frank Sayer Graham substantially extended Heather Cottage, and the interior was transformed into a spacious Arts and Crafts house. This movement was at the height of its popularity between 1880 and 1910 and its advocates, led by William Morris, concentrated on the decorative and applied arts and championed the need to produce practical but aesthetically pleasing household fabric and furnishings.⁶⁹ Heather Cottage was fitted out with beautiful stained glass windows, colourful tiled fireplaces and a magnificent oak staircase, all of which are retained to this day.

Sadly, soon after the completion of the fashionable alterations, Frank's personal life was to change dramatically as his wife Mary died on 28th December 1911, aged only 45, and was buried with his parents in Aysgarth churchyard. Frank was actively involved in his parish church all his life, and in her memory he presented a beautiful intricately carved oak pulpit to St Andrew's Church, Aysgarth, which was installed in 1915, and which still graces the nave today.⁷⁰ The pulpit was carved by Ralph Hedley, who had been born near Richmond but went on to become famous as a Newcastle-based woodcarver and painter of scenes of everyday life,⁷¹ and so it would seem that this was a generous gift of great value. It is also clear that it was of great emotional significance to Frank as, after the personal details, the carved inscription reads "She sweetened the lives of others and in their love survives".

Oak pulpit in memory of Frank's first wife, Aysgarth Church.

Carved inscription on the pulpit, Aysgarth Church.

That Frank had chosen a very suitable way to memorialise Mary is revealed by a codicil to his will, written in 1925, in which he left to his second wife "such furniture as was carved or worked by the gentle hands of my late wife, including a corner cupboard, a mirror and a table with initials thereon".[72] The wording of this bequest suggests that Mary may have been actively involved in the Arts and Crafts movement via her woodworking hobby. At the end of the nineteenth century, Beatrice Carpenter, the wife of the then owner of Kiplin Hall, near Richmond, was connected with the movement through the work of the Home Arts and Industries Association. This society aimed to revive traditional crafts such as woodcarving and metalwork by running evening classes for people of humble origins, the one associated with Kiplin being held at Bolton-on-Swale. Beatrice Carpenter herself was a very talented woodcarver and it is intriguing to wonder if Mary knew her and visited Kiplin, where a number of pieces of beautifully inlaid and carved furniture can still be seen today.[73]

Frank and his second wife, Annie

It is said locally that Mary asked Frank to take care of her sister, Annie, after her death and he did this by making her his second wife. Reading between the lines of his original will of 1917[74] and the six subsequent codicils made between 1925 and 1941, it would seem that Frank's second marriage may have been entered into mainly out of duty rather than love, as only part of his estate was left to Annie. In his first codicil of 1925, perhaps in order to justify his decisions on her inheritance, he wrote "I wish to record my conviction that my wife . . . will not after my death desire to reside in Aysgarth . . . and any provision made by me for her . . . is based

Annie weeding in the Rock Garden (Rock Garden Archive).

on that opinion".[75] This may seem strange, but Mary had left Frank a cottage that she still owned in Wales,[76] which he, in his will bequeathed to Annie, and perhaps expected her to move to if he died first. In the end, although the codicils reveal that he kept changing his mind as to the details, Frank retained the bequest of the Welsh cottage to Annie but also left her Blades Cottage, another property he owned in Aysgarth, as well as some personal and family items, a sum to be taken as money or goods, and curiously, his "Hoover Sweeper".[77]

Frank's bequests to St Andrew's Church, Aysgarth

One decision that Frank did not rethink after the original will was written was that Heather Cottage, its contents and land, including the Rock Garden, were to be sold in order to fund a number of public and private bequests. Some of these were to friends and relatives, which, again, he sometimes altered or revoked as time went on, but the most generous of his bequests were to St Andrew's Church, which shows how dear he held it throughout his long life. Although in his last codicil of 1941 he had to revoke an earlier bequest to the sexton to look after the graves of Aysgarth residents "in view of the financial situation brought about by the present war",[78] he retained his earlier instructions for a trust fund to be created from the residue of his estate which was to be divided into two moieties to benefit the church. The first half was to be invested in order to provide an annual income to pay for the services of a curate or lay reader "in order to forever bring additional religious and spiritual comfort to the parishioners",[79] and I understand that this is still in operation today within the Penhill Benefice. The second half was to be realised with a substantial sum to be used to pay for an "elaborate and handsome" tablet to record that the bequest was in memory of his first wife, and the remainder allocated for "the beautifying" of St Andrew's Church internally via woodwork, either for re-flooring or re-seating. The brass plaque, erected after Frank's death and memorialising the trust fund, can still be seen on the north wall of the nave, but unfortunately it does not have details of the changes that were made to the church fabric in Mary's name.

Frank's later life in Aysgarth

Frank standing in the Rock Garden (Rock Garden Archive).

As the twentieth century progressed, garments made from real fur became less popular, with the result that Frank's game dealing business became mainly concerned with the sale of live grouse for export. The income generated from this trade enabled him to acquire more property and land in Aysgarth and he created plantations of trees around the village which survive today. It is said locally that he had a private nursery next door to Heather Cottage at the house known then as Rose Cottage and now as Spring Hill. A newspaper obituary written shortly after his death drew attention to his interest in all things horticultural, stating that

Herbert Robinson, Frank's gardener handyman (Rock Garden Archive).

"gardening was his special hobby, his giant rock garden opposite his residence and his fields of tulips, being the centres of attraction".[80] A postcard showing a photograph of Aysgarth, probably taken during the 1930s, in which the Rock Garden is visible, shows that it still looked in pristine condition. It is said locally that Herbert Robinson, a self-employed gardener handyman who lived in nearby Newbiggin, Bishopdale, worked for Frank for two days a week at this time.

Frank could look across from his bedroom at the front of Heather Cottage and see the waterfall area of the Rock Garden, and this view must have given him great pleasure, particularly towards the end of his life. Arthur Mee's description of Aysgarth in *The King's England*, written in 1941, when Frank would have been 82, confirms that the garden was still a delight at that date:

> The village has lovely old houses with creepered [*sic*] walls, but it has nothing more charming than a rock garden by the green-banked wayside, where the grey rocks, looking like crags of the fells, are a dazzling mosaic of colour with hundreds of ferns and flowers growing in their crannies.[81]

Postcard of Aysgarth, c.1930s (Rock Garden Archive).

Close reading of the newspaper obituary mentioned above shows that Frank well deserved its headline, "Public service to Wensleydale". In addition to stating that he was a survivor of the original trustees of Aysgarth Institute, which opened in 1907, the article described him as:

> a lifelong resident of Aysgarth, where he was a highly esteemed personality, and had an outstanding record of public service. Mr Graham served Aysgarth Parish Church as a churchwarden for many years; he was a Justice of the Peace and member of the North Riding County Council for nine years and served on the Aysgarth Rural Council as chairman and a member for Aysgarth for 24 years. He was keenly interested in young people and education and for years he was a Governor and chairman of the Governors of Yorebridge Grammar School [in Bainbridge], the Graham Cup, which he presented for the most upright pupil, being annually presented.[82]

Frank's funeral at St Andrew's Church, Aysgarth

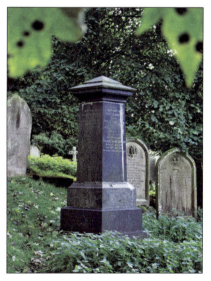

Sayer Graham monument in Aysgarth churchyard.

Frank died on 30th June 1946 at Heather Cottage, aged 87, and was buried in Aysgarth churchyard with the rest of his family. A handsome granite monument ordered by him in 1925 from Priestmans, Monumental Sculptors of Darlington,[83] and inscribed with family names on three of its four sides, marks the spot. The newspaper obituary gives a good indication of his standing in the local community and wider area as it reveals that well over one hundred mourners paid their respects at his funeral at St Andrew's Church, which took the form of a choral service led by the vicar, the Rev E.D. Deane, with Miss Blades playing the organ. In addition to his widow, Annie, and other relatives, the names of Doris Levill, his last maid, and Herbert Robinson, his gardener handyman, both appear in the list of "chief mourners". Many of the principal residents of the district and friends from Aysgarth and further afield also attended, as did representatives of the official bodies on which Frank had served.[84]

Memorial tablet to Dr Will Pickles, Aysgarth Church.

For me, one name in particular that stands out in the list of mourners is that of Dr Will Pickles of Aysgarth, who may well have been the physician in attendance during Frank's final days. Dr Pickles had served the community of mid-Wensleydale since 1912 as a General Practitioner, a role he would continue to fulfil until the 1960s, but he was no ordinary family doctor.[85] At the age of 42, helped by his family, he started to meticulously record details of the incidence and spread of infectious disease in Aysgarth and the villages close by, and thereby carried out ground-breaking research. The results were published in 1939 in *Epidemiology in Country Practice*,[86] which became a classic book on the subject, and many honours followed. Dr Pickle's bungalow, Town Ends, which he had built just beyond the eastern end of Aysgarth village, became a mecca for medical visitors and in 1953 he took on the important role of first president of the newly formed Royal College of General Practitioners.

The end of an era

Following Frank's death, his wife Annie did not leave the area as he had predicted, but continued to live in Aysgarth. However, Heather Cottage and its associated land, including the Rock Garden, were indeed sold, and the catalogue for the public auction, held in June

1947, of all the furniture, pictures and other contents consists of long lists of possessions detailed room by room, hinting at considerable wealth.[87] Frank's business and leisure interests are laid bare as books on grouse, dogs, birds, and, of course, gardening are included. None are named but it may be that a copy of the 1907 version of Mr Clark's *Alpine Plants*, with its mention of Heather Cottage, was amongst their number. The auction lists also reveal that in the garage numerous cast zinc plant labels remained, and perhaps these were similar to several discovered in recent years hidden in crevices in the Rock Garden, identical in design to Acme ones illustrated in an advert in the Backhouse alpine catalogue of 1911. Many other gardening related items including tools and rockery stone were also to be included in the auction, all standing as poignant testament to Frank's lifetime passion for horticulture.

In addition to his other interests Frank was a keen naturalist,[88] and a quotation from the start of a letter he wrote to *The Northern Echo* in

Heather Cottage contents auction catalogue cover (Rock Garden Archive).

Cast zinc plant labels found in the Rock Garden.

November 1938, with the headline "Swallows and House Martins in Wensleydale", gives a hint of his character in later life, and provides a fitting end to the story of the creation of the Rock Garden:

> As a bird lover, and one greatly indebted to birds, I should like to say how much I appreciate the Out-of-Doors Diary of your correspondent C.H.R. He daily serves up something elevating, something to lift our minds and hearts above politics, the preparations for war, death and destruction. Some paragraph of his is bound to divert the minds of all nature lovers from the fear of war to the beautiful things of the countryside in which we live so peacefully . . .[89]

Frank's fears were realised as he lived long enough to witness the death and destruction of the Second World War, but he would surely be glad to know that Wensleydale has remained a place where one can still live "peacefully", and his beloved Rock Garden, one of his "beautiful things of the countryside", has not only survived, but has been restored to its former glory. In the next chapter I begin the second story, that of re-creation, by charting the decline of the garden during the latter part of the twentieth century.

CHAPTER SIX

A QUIRKY WILDERNESS: THE ROCK GARDEN IN DECLINE

Sir Charles Isham and garden gnomes

Frank's death brought about the end of the association of the Sayer Graham family with the Aysgarth Rock Garden, and during the second half of the twentieth century it was bought and sold a number of times, and at least once was in separate ownership from Heather Cottage. Although successive owners maintained the Rock Garden to the best of their ability, local residents remember it as overgrown, one describing it as a "quirky wilderness". This was certainly an apt description for the period during the 1980s when it became part of a business venture to display and sell garden gnomes, and some of these plaster models can still be seen lurking in crevices with their paint faded and, curiously, mostly headless.

Headless gnome found in the Rock Garden.

The history of garden gnomes, loved or detested in equal measure, is a fascinating one which links into the story of rock gardening. Sir

Charles Isham of Lamport, Northamptonshire, an eccentric landowner and gardener, built a large rockery near his house in 1847.[90] On a visit to Nuremberg in Germany soon afterwards he discovered that the miners believed that tiny gnome-like beings led them by lights and knocking to the best seams of minerals. Sir Charles found hand-modelled terracotta figures of gnomes for sale and brought a large number back with him to populate his rockwork. He placed them, with props such as spades and wheelbarrows, to give the impression, on an appropriate scale, that they were mining the rocks and also included doggerel verses to entertain visitors when he opened the grounds for charity. It is believed that, as these miniature rockery adornments were already in place by the 1860s, they may well have been the earliest introduction of gnomes into an English garden, and the interest created by Sir Charles Isham must have surely played its part in the development of the Victorian fashion for rock gardening.

The decline of rock gardening

As the twentieth century progressed alpine gardening declined in importance within the world of horticulture, and this lessening of interest may have been a factor in the gradual demise of the Aysgarth Rock Garden after Frank Sayer Graham died. The first RHS Chelsea Flower Show was held in May 1913, and in its early days all the major alpine nurseries, including James Backhouse and Son, created rockeries that were considered the most prestigious type of show gardens on display.[91] However, as time went on, and particularly after the Second World War, other less time-consuming styles of gardening became more fashionable, with the result that, although the specialist societies continued to provide for the needs of enthusiasts, there have been relatively few rock gardens on display at Chelsea during the last forty years. In fact in the gardens of the large country houses the decline set in as early as the First World War, once there was less manpower available to tend high maintenance rockeries. Difficulties continued in the post-war period as landowners faced greater tax burdens and consequent decline in their financial security. As time went on there were also great changes in the specialist nursery trade due to increased competition from companies selling cheap packets of seeds, and these factors, taken alongside the difficult national economic climate, meant that many firms experienced problems.

The demise of the Backhouse firm

In the case of James Backhouse and Son, decline set in even before the outbreak of the First World War. As described in Chapter Two, the firm became a limited liability company in 1891 and it would seem that financial problems then began quite quickly. According to census records, no members of the family lived at West Bank after the early 1890s and in about 1910 the house and some of the grounds, including the famous rock garden, were sold by James III to his friend Sir James Hamilton, who was head of the Yorkshire Insurance Company.[92] It must have been a great disappointment to the Backhouse firm when in 1910 their tender to construct the enormous sandstone rock garden at the RHS Garden at Wisley was one of several rejected, and that of James Pulham and Son, the firm mentioned in Chapter One whose fame had originally rested on artificial rock, was chosen instead.[93]

Adverts for James Backhouse and Son included in the Aysgarth show schedule of 1909, mentioned in Chapter Four, reveal that a retail branch was open in the centre of Leeds at that time. Perhaps this was a last ditch effort to extend the market, but it would seem not to have been enough to revive the ailing fortunes of the firm. The financial deterioration continued, and at some point liquidators were appointed with the result that in 1921 the business was put up for sale and was bought by Sir James Hamilton who headed a consortium of investors. The nursery did continue to trade, and to add a local note, a letter in the Rock Garden Archive, written in 2002 by the renowned historian of the Dales, Marie Hartley, then in her mid-nineties, relates how she visited the nursery at York frequently when living in Wetherby as a young woman and states how she remembered the expert gardeners there.

When Sir James died in 1935, by the terms of his will, West Bank House and its private gardens were sold to York Corporation with the proviso that Lady Hamilton could continue to live there as a tenant for her lifetime.[94] During Sir James' ownership of the nursery the grounds had not been opened to the public, although sometimes local groups and charities were allowed to hold events there at weekends. However, this situation was to change after he died as he had decided that part of the land should become a public open space for the citizens of York to enjoy, and the result was that West Bank Park was created and opened in July 1938. The rock garden remained in the private family grounds close to the house, although after Lady Hamilton's death in 1945 these areas also became part of the public park once the paths had been improved.

The Backhouse nursery continued as a business enterprise in some form until 1955, but in November of that year it finally closed and a grand auction of the plant stock was held which attracted both private individuals and professional growers.[95] The land was sold to York Corporation and, despite conditions which stated that the gardens should be added to West Bank Park and the rest of the former nursery area kept as fields, much was used for housing, and any open ground became neglected and overgrown. In the late 1960s the area that had been the rock garden became part of York Council's nursery when it relocated from Fulford. In order to create a flat area and thereby increase useable space, most of the large rocks were driven into the former lake over the winter of 1972-3, and thus any remaining vestige of its former glory was destroyed.[96] Around this time the now disused West Bank House, which had become a target for vandals, was demolished, and

The entrance to West Bank Park, York.

so little physical evidence of the Backhouse era was left. Some of the park did remain open, and when in the 1990s local people heard that a possible housing development was threatening its future, a campaign was launched with the result that the impact was minimised, and a Friends group formed which has remained active ever since.

Although this is a depressing story, I am pleased to report that on a visit to the park in June 2013 I discovered a well-cared-for twenty acre urban space with ghostly vestiges of the Backhouse nursery show gardens remaining. Around the gated entrance at the south end and in the northern half, where West Bank House was situated, many specimen trees, including giant redwoods, can be seen. Even more poignantly, in one small wooded and somewhat overgrown corner near Acomb Road, some large stones, which may be from the famous rock garden, have been formed into a small rockery and a modest plaque commemorates the firm. There, luxuriant ferns and even a bamboo are to be found and it is possible that some of these are relic plants from the Backhouse era.

The rockery, West Bank Park, York.

Mr Clark's later life

In view of the decline and eventual demise of the Backhouse firm, it is interesting to wonder what became of Mr Clark, and although I have no definitive proof, it would appear that soon after he was connected with the Aysgarth Rock Garden he began to work on his own account. A newspaper article of 1905[97] reveals that he was remanded in September of that year on the charge of making false entries in time sheets while working for James Backhouse and Son, but no evidence of a trial or its verdict has come to light to date, which suggests that the case was dropped. Whatever the outcome, the allegation must have meant that relations were irrevocably damaged between him and his employer and it seems likely he would have left the firm sooner or later. There is evidence that points in that direction when the two editions of his book, *Alpine Plants*, are compared. Mr Clark ended his 1901 preface with the address, "The Nurseries, York", but in 1907 this has been removed and the photographs of the famous rockery and its alpine plants have also disappeared, as has an advert for James Backhouse and Son that was included at the back of the first edition. In fact the wording of the descriptive part of the 1907 frontispiece, referred to in Chapter Four, makes me wonder if he produced the second edition of his book as a marketing tool for a new self-employed business venture:

Mr W.A. Clark, Jasmine House, Bishopthorpe Road, York,

Is prepared to undertake and carry out <u>all work</u> in connection with Alpine Rockwork, the laying out of Water Gardens, the construction of Japanese Gardens, and the general arrangement of Grounds; providing all necessary material for the construction and stocking of the work undertaken; and all labour, by competent men, to carry it out.

Mr Clark is confident that his long and large experience in this class of work will enable him to give entire satisfaction. He is also prepared to advise in respect to the selection of plants of all kinds for special positions, soils, or climates. In every case it will be Mr

Clark's especial endeavour to regulate all estimates given, so that efficient results may be obtained at reasonable cost.[98]

In addition, Mr Clark provided prizes in his own right for the 1909 Aysgarth show, as described in Chapter Four, but he made no mention of a Backhouse connection, despite the fact that there were several adverts for the firm's products within the brochure. This may well be further evidence of his changed employment status and confirmation seems to be provided by *Kelly's Directory of North and East Ridings and York* of 1909 which lists his occupation simply as "gardener". He had also moved house and was now living at 78, Bishopthorpe Road, York – presumably the property named as "Jasmine House" in the frontispiece of the 1907 book.

Although away from home, perhaps working on a garden, at the time of the 1911 census, the details reveal that Mr Clark was still living on Bishopthorpe Road with his wife, Mary Louisa, then aged 39, whom he had married in York during the summer of 1892. The records show that at that time there were six children at home including the eldest, John William Angus, who was 18 and working as a railway clerk. In 2013 I had the privilege of examining a copy of the 1901 edition of *Alpine Plants* which bears the hand-written dedication "Presented to Jn Wm Angus Clark by his father the Author, Febr 1906". John William Angus would have been about 12 years old, and as that was the school leaving age at the time, perhaps the book was given to him as a token to mark the transition to manhood when he began his working life. In addition to John, the family

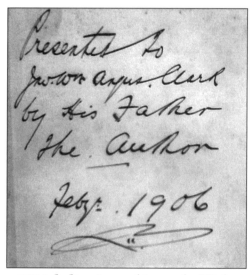

1906 dedication to his son by W.A. Clark in *Alpine Plants*, 1901 edition.

also included Tom, the boy who had written the postcard mentioned in Chapter Four, who was now 14 years old and still at school, three daughters and a baby son.

The next details available for Mr Clark appear in *Kelly's Directory of West Riding* of 1912 and show that at that date he was a "landscape gardener" living in Dringhouses, then a village on the outskirts of York not far from his former workplace at Holgate. Two newspaper cuttings stuck into his son's copy of the 1901 book reveal that Mr Clark lived in that community for the rest of his life at an address given as "The Nurseries", but examinations of old maps and trade directories have not brought forth details of what or where this was. It would seem that Mr Clark's reputation was not tarnished by his brush with the law in 1905 as he continued to be recognised as a well-known authority in his field, as evidenced by a newspaper article in the *Yorkshire Herald* of 1922. This described, along with a photograph, how he had forwarded a presentation copy of the 1907 edition of his book, specially bound in morocco leather, to Princess Mary, the Princess Royal, on the occasion of her marriage to Viscount Lascelles, later 6th Earl of Harewood.[99] Similarly an obituary in the *Yorkshire Gazette*, composed soon after his death on 1st February 1950, aged 94, reveals that he was still held in high repute in his profession in old age, as he was described as a "leading figure in the gardening world, being a specialist in landscape gardening".[100]

The Rock Garden under threat

The above discussion of Mr Clark's later life is something of a digression and once again it is time to draw attention back to the Aysgarth Rock Garden. Towards the end of the 1980s there was a danger that the plot on which it stands would be sold for development, and the local community were outraged at the prospect of the rocks being removed and the garden thereby destroyed. English Heritage became involved and the Rock Garden's national significance within the history of horticulture was recognised, the outcome being that it was granted Grade II Listed status on 4th February 1988. People tend to assume that the listing refers to the garden, but in fact it is the built stone structures and iron railings that are protected by legislation for posterity.

Soon after this, the garden was brought back into the ownership of Heather Cottage, and when the property was bought by Angela and Peter Jauneika in 1998, they discovered that they had accidentally become the owners of a listed rock garden, which by then was very overgrown with self-sown trees, brambles and weeds. For a while they tried unsuccessfully to tame the wilderness in their spare time, but soon Angela realised that the task of restoration was beyond what they could do themselves. She decided that a major project with outside funding would be the only way to proceed and in the final chapter I tell the remarkable story of how the Rock Garden was re-created at the start of the twenty-first century.

CHAPTER SEVEN

AN OPEN ROCK GARDEN: THE STORY OF RE-CREATION

Angela Jauneika's vision

The overgrown Rock Garden before restoration
(Rock Garden Archive).

Soon after arriving in Aysgarth, Angela Jauneika discovered via a chance encounter with an academic expert that the Rock Garden was considered to be of great historical importance as a rare surviving example of the Backhouse construction style. This was the trigger she needed to make her absolutely determined to find a way to restore it to its former glory. However, her vision of re-creation was that it should become an "open rock garden" for local residents and visitors to enjoy – a very different role from its private past. By talking to local and garden historians and visiting various record offices and archives, over time Angela amassed many useful original documents, press reports and old photographs. It was disappointing though, that despite her best efforts, no planting details or construction plans came to light to inform the restoration. However, the biggest challenge by far was that connected with finding outside funding for the project, a task that Angela embarked on with a huge amount of dedication and hard work. If she had not had such a clear vision of what she wanted to achieve she would surely have given up, but she persisted in her quest, and after three-and-a-half years of writing unsuccessful grant applications, her luck changed.

Funding the project

Angela had estimated that the total cost of the restoration work would be about £25,000, and to her delight, in 2002 The Yorkshire Dales Millennium Trust (YDMT) agreed to provide an eighty per cent grant, funded by the Heritage Lottery Fund. The remaining money was then raised from smaller grants, including one from the RHS Coke Fund specifically for replanting. Local people also responded generously by donating money and the Jauneikas themselves personally made up any financial shortfall. The Yorkshire Dales National Park Authority showed their support by offering to provide consultancy services without charge, but even when all the funds were in place, the stress did not end as the YDMT grant came with conditions attached. For the money to be received the restoration had to be completed within six months, and this meant that all the work had to take place over the winter of 2002-3. This was a real challenge but in the end a month's extension was agreed which enabled the replanting to take place at a more appropriate time during the following spring. Angela soon discovered that the project was taking over her life, particularly as every step of the restoration was recorded for posterity during periodic filming by Tyne Tees Television, the outcome being a two-part ITV documentary entitled *The Secret Garden* which was first shown in September 2003.

The restoration of the Rock Garden

It was clear that expert advice was needed on all aspects of the restoration and garden historian and designer, Jo Makin of Harrogate, was commissioned to draw up a report which outlined a proposed programme of work of clearance, maintenance and replanting.[101] However, before any of this could be put into practice, it was essential that the structural soundness of the Rock Garden was checked and so a detailed survey was carried out by Capstone Consulting Engineers of Leeds.[102] Their opinion was that although a small amount of remedial work was needed, overall the rockwork had remained in a remarkably stable condition despite the years of neglect.

Once the necessary structural repairs had been completed, the next task was to fell the self-seeded ash and sycamore trees and chemically treat the stumps to prevent regrowth. Only then could the main job of clearance of shrubby plants and weeds that choked the whole area begin in earnest. A number of firms tendered for the work and Michael Myers of Smelthouses Nursery, near Harrogate, was chosen because of his experience and expertise in the area of alpines, and he and his father started the mammoth task in October 2002. The job took six full weeks to complete, and during this time it became clear that there had once been a cascade running down to the stream-like rill, and after lead pipes were discovered it was possible to work out that the feature had originally been spring fed. As there was no sign of the original source of the water, it was decided to lay on a mains supply so that a closed system powered by an electric pump could be installed. Much work was then carried out in order to ensure that the cascade area and base and sides of the rill were reasonably watertight, but even so remedial repairs have been necessary over the years because of the porous nature of limestone. The stone walls on the boundaries of the Rock Garden also needed to be repaired during the restoration project, with one ten-metre section having to be completely rebuilt, and similarly the iron railings and gate at the front needed urgent attention, but fortunately the expenses involved were covered by the YDMT grant.

Once the restoration of the hard landscaping was complete, it was time to restock the Rock Garden with new plants. Jo Makin had suggested that, given the absence of original details, rather than limit the species to those that were available in the early twentieth century, the planting should remain true to the spirit of Edwardian times but could contain modern, more robust cultivars of lime tolerant alpines. She also suggested that the most effective visual impact would be created by turning the "normal" way of planting a rock garden on its head, so that smaller plants were on the lower levels at eye level and larger more showy plants higher up.

The rear of the Rock Garden soon after restoration (Rock Garden Archive).

By April 2003 Michael Myers, assisted by Angela, had completed the huge task of planting about 2,000 alpines, shrubs and small conifers and photographs show that the design looked effective from the outset. That arrangement of plants is still essentially in place today, although in recent years a number of common species that had become somewhat rampant have been removed and replaced with less vigorous varieties. Jo Makin's original vision for the former vegetable garden was to create an alpine meadow planted with bulbs and wild flowers, perhaps inspired by the one close to the rock garden at RHS Wisley. This was to constitute a second phase of the restoration but was not in the end realised. Instead the area was developed into a pleasing combination of lawn and perennial borders with graceful birches and a variety of shrubs.

The reopening of the Rock Garden

Angela Jauneika and Eric Robson at the reopening ceremony, July 2003 (Rock Garden Archive).

Thanks to the dedication of all involved, the deadline imposed by the funders for completion of the restoration was met and the Rock Garden was officially reopened on 5th July 2003. Over fifty invited guests and villagers attended a memorable afternoon of celebrations and Angela was fortunate to secure the services of Eric Robson, host of BBC Radio 4's *Gardeners' Question Time*, to perform the opening ceremony. However, perhaps the most important guest, because of her link with Frank Sayer Graham, was the now elderly Doris Biggs (nee Levill), his last maid. In a letter in the Rock Garden Archive, written to thank Angela after the day, she expressed her delight at seeing the "rockery once again in all its glory" and her pleasure in being given "a wonderful afternoon of nostalgia".

From 2003 onwards Angela, assisted by her husband and a part-time gardener, maintained the Rock Garden to a high standard, and, true to her intentions, it remained freely open to all. Due to the publicity generated by the television documentary, magazine articles, press reports and word of mouth amongst alpine enthusiasts, the garden became better and better known, leading to a steady stream of visitors over the years.

In 2011 Angela and Peter decided that the time had come to sell, and my husband and I, who often visited the garden, decided that the chance of owning such an important piece of horticultural history was an opportunity we should not let slip from our grasp. We were lucky enough to have our offer to purchase accepted, with the result that we took over as owners at the end of January 2012 just as the snowdrops and aconites in the borders at the rear of the garden began to flower.

AFTERWORD

Adrian and Rosemary Anderson, new owners of the Rock Garden, February 2012.

In the time that my husband and I have owned the Aysgarth Rock Garden, whilst mindful of the responsibility we have taken on, we have gained an enormous amount of pleasure and satisfaction from it. We have also discovered how much it means to people, local residents and Dales visitors alike. It seems to exert an emotional appeal quite out of scale with its modest size, and clearly is seen as a very special place by many. This was really brought home to us during the weekend of the Queen's Diamond Jubilee in June 2012 when we arrived to do some maintenance work and inadvertently witnessed a marriage proposal taking place in traditional fashion on bended knee, with ring proffered. As family members of the bride-to-be had been primed and were also present, there was no awkwardness on our part, but rather a feeling of pride that the Rock Garden had been chosen as the backdrop for such a special moment in a young couple's life. Emotion certainly ran high that day, as by a quirk of fate, our younger daughter had announced her engagement the day before.

Without Angela's vision and determination there is no doubt that this "private rock garden" would have been lost for ever, and we feel very privileged that we were chosen to be the people to develop it further as an "open rock garden" that welcomes visitors freely all year round. Although in the eyes of the law we are the owners, in reality we consider ourselves no more than temporary custodians of its ancient rockwork and ever changing flora. Our hope is that the Rock Garden will continue to delight people for many generations to come for, as Donna E. Schaper writes in her book *The Art of Spiritual Rock Gardening*:

> The uses of the rock garden as a site of beauty, reflection and spiritual nourishment are many. Building a quiet corner of stones and plants slowly and meditatively over time is its true meaning. Process over product, journey over destination, forever a work in progress – rock is the best metaphor that we have for everlastingness.[103]

APPENDIX

THE ROCK GARDEN TODAY: A DESCRIPTIVE GUIDE BY A. ANDERSON

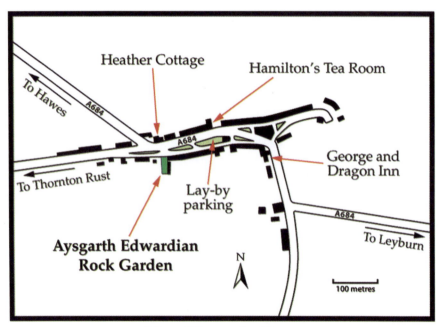

Map of Aysgarth village.

Introduction

The Aysgarth Rock Garden is to be found adjacent to the main A684 road opposite Heather Cottage at the western end of the village. It occupies a 0.14 acre walled site measuring approximately 14 by 42 metres, and lies at about 230 metres above sea level.

The garden is open throughout the year, but unfortunately is not suitable for disabled or wheelchair access due to narrow and uneven paths and steps. Visitors enter at their own risk and are requested to keep to the paths and to be aware of low stone lintels, open water and other potential hazards. If visiting by car please do not park directly outside the garden but use the lay-by indicated on the above map or other parking within the village.

There is no entrance charge but any donation towards the upkeep and development of the garden is greatly appreciated – please use the donations box by the entrance.

This descriptive guide divides the garden into several named and numbered areas. To help appreciate the layout, the area numbers are detailed on the plan below.

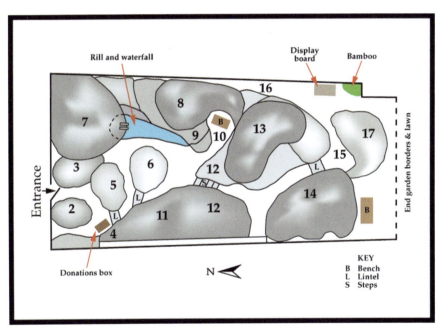

Plan of Aysgarth Rock Garden.

Outside the garden

Picea glauca var. albertina 'Conica' **beyond the entrance gate.**

Outside the entrance to the garden is a grass verge that has been planted with *Narcissus obvallaris* (Tenby daffodil) and crocuses, making a fine show in early spring. In view, just inside the gate to the left side of the path, is *Picea glauca var. albertina 'Conica'* and to the right *Berberis darwinii* – likely survivors of original plantings within the garden. Looking towards the higher sections of the garden specimens of *Pinus mugo var. pumilio* will be seen, some of which have been underplanted with bergenias.

The garden entrance (2, 3 & 5)

Attached to the railings, to the left of the gate, is an information plaque giving background information about the garden and the 2002-3 restoration. Beyond the entrance gate a gravel path leads past the donations box and beneath the first lintel. Within crevices of the rocks

Asplenium trichomanes and *Asplenium ceterach*.

Erythronium 'Pagoda'.

Cyclamen mirabile.

View through the first lintel towards the donations box and garden entrance.

Colchicum agrippinum.

close by the left side of the path, and indeed scattered throughout the garden, are small native ferns, for example: *Asplenium ceterach* (rusty back fern), *Asplenium trichomanes* (maidenhair spleenwort) and *Asplenium scolopendrium* (hart's tongue fern). Cyclamen, pulsatilla and primroses are planted at the foot of the rocks and within the open area to the left side of the path. The area on the right hand side adjacent to the donations box and beneath the berberis is carpeted in the springtime by drifts of *Erythronium 'Pagoda'* and in the autumn by *Colchicum agrippinum*.

Beyond the first lintel (5)

Beyond the first lintel there is a choice of paths – one by the side of the western boundary rockwork that continues to the second lintel and the other that turns left immediately beyond the first lintel and leads towards the stream-like rill and cascade. At eye level, the planting within the rockwork on the left hand side of this second path includes saxifrages, sempervivums, violas and sedums. At a higher level aubrieta and alyssum mingle with the lower branches of a *Pinus mugo*.

Aubrieta with
Pinus mugo var. pumilio.

Saxifraga 'Francis Cade'.

Sempervivum 'Café'.

The rill, cascade and backdrop (8 & 9)

The path by the northern boundary leads to the edge of the stream-like rill with its backdrop of the cascade and associated plantings. The cascade runs for a few minutes each time the movement sensor near the entrance is triggered; the damp environment thus created on the slope ensures a good display of *Primula denticulata* each spring. Ferns, spring bulbs, including *Fritillaria meleagris,* and geraniums flourish. During June two orchids *Dactylorhiza 'Bressingham Bonus'* and *Dactylorhiza elata* give an impressive display. The rill is planted with a variety of oxygenating and marginal plants including *Caltha palustris* (marsh marigold).

Fritillaria meleagris.

Please note that the cascade does not run during the winter months.

Caltha palustris **within the rill.**

The cascade and backdrop, photographed from outside the front garden.

Papaver atlanticum growing from rock crevices above the rill.

Close up of the cascade.

The central rocky projection (6)

This rockwork lies immediately behind the path adjacent to the rill. The sunny south side provides an ideal home for several sempervivums whilst the top has been planted with varieties of polypodium ferns – at their best during August and September when other ferns are beginning to fade. Self-seeded specimens of *Erinus alpinus* (fairy foxglove) pepper the rockwork.

The western boundary rockwork up to the steps (11&12)

This area can be viewed from the path that leads from the first lintel to the steps via the second lintel. Planting within this boundary rockwork includes *Cotoneaster horizontalis*, varieties of cistus, *Euphorbia characias* and hellebores. During September Japanese anemones planted high up are at their best.

Cotoneaster horizontalis **and Japanese anemones within the western boundary rockwork.**

View from the edge of the rill towards the steps with the central rocky projection to the right.

View towards the dell from the second lintel.

Polystichum setiferum 'Plumosomultilobum' at the entrance to the dell.

Primula marginata.

Cardamine kitaibelii.

The dell (10)

Asarina procumbens.

This small area is enclosed on three sides by rocky cliffs – those on the south side are the highest in the garden. *Cerastium tomentosum* (snow-in-summer) and *Asarina procumbens* (trailing snapdragon) cascade from these high rocks. Asarina is a vigorous self-seeder and would take over the garden if permitted. The moist, shady environment of the dell is a perfect home for the early flowers of *Primula marginata* and *Cardamine kitaibelii*. Later in the year *Saxifraga callosa* produces 30cm long, low-arching and densely flowered one-sided wands of pure white flowers – an impressive sight.

Anemone ranunculoides semi-plena.

Before the third lintel (13 & 14)

Leaving the dell, a path continues via rough steps to a gorge-like area of the garden, with high rockwork on both sides. On the left is a specimen of *Osmanthus delavayi* and during May the area beneath this is carpeted with the fresh green foliage and bright yellow flowers of *Anemone ranunculoides semi-plena*. Later in the year an astrantia and geraniums provide colour. The path continues beneath the third lintel and into the fernery.

View from the top of the steps into the dell.

The fernery (15)

On entering the fernery the spidery branches of a huge overhead juniper are immediately apparent. During 2012 a selection of ferns was planted within this area, especially chosen to be able to survive the conditions of dry shade created by the juniper. Continuing along the path beyond the fernery, a garden information board will be seen on the left and next to this an unknown bamboo, thought to have been planted at the time of development of the original garden.

The southern extent of the rockwork (14 & 17)

The path continues around a rocky mound, planted with saxifrages, sedums and campanulas, before reaching a garden bench and above this the high southern rockwork. *Alyssum saxatile* thrives in these dry, sunny conditions – the sweetly-scented, lemon-coloured flowers are a fine sight in spring.

View of the south wall from the end garden.

View towards the third lintel and fernery with juniper above.

The end garden

Aconites and snowdrops beneath *Betula ermanii 'Grayswood Hill'*.

This is a small lawned area with borders on two sides. These borders are a mass of snowdrops and aconites in early spring which then disappear beneath the foliage of perennial plants as the year progresses. Arising from the borders are the following trees: in the south-west corner three *Betula ermanii 'Grayswood Hill'*, opposite these a specimen of *Sorbus fruticulosa* and adjacent to the path *Prunus padus 'Pandora'*. Of the herbaceous plants and bulbs within the borders mention must be made of the fine *Lilium 'Mrs R.O. Backhouse'*, with its purple-speckled, mustard-coloured flowers – a fitting plant for a Backhouse garden.

Gardens evolve over time, none more so than the Rock Garden, where the demise of some plants and the need to replant or redevelop sections of the garden mean that this descriptive guide is but a snapshot. We hope that readers of this book will be able to visit and enjoy the garden as it changes through the seasons and develops over the years.

For further pictures of the garden and more detailed planting lists please visit www.aysgarthrockgarden.co.uk

REFERENCES

Foreword

1. L. Hawthorne, "Uncovering a rocky past", *The Garden*, 140, 4 (April 2005), pp.260-263.

2. English Heritage Grade II Listing for Aysgarth Edwardian Rock Garden, 1988. http://list.english-heritage.org.uk/resultsingle.aspx?uid=1131982 (last accessed 1.2.14)

Chapter One

3. H.N.H., "A beautiful rock garden", *The Garden*, 12.6.1875, pp.477- 478.

4. N. Shulman, *A Rage for Rock Gardening* (Short Books, 2002), p.44.

5. B. Elliott, *The British Rock Garden in the Twentieth Century*, Occasional Papers from the RHS Lindley Library, number 6 (RHS, 2011).

6. G.S. Thomas, *The Rock Garden and its Plants: from grotto to alpine house* (Sagapress Inc., 1989).

7. *Ibid.* p.31.

8. F.S. Heath, *Garden Rockery: how to make, plant and manage it* (George Routledge and Sons Ltd, 1908).

9. English Heritage, *Durability Guaranteed: Pulhamite rockwork, its conservation and repair* (EH, 2008).

10. T. Musgrave, C. Gardner and W. Musgrave, *The Plant Hunters* (Ward Lock, 1998).

11. P. Westland, *Terrariums* (The Apple Press, 1993).

12. W. Robinson, *Alpine Flowers for Gardens*, 3rd Edition (John Murray, 1903).

13. *Ibid.* p.x.

Chapter Two

14. Article on Backhouse family, *Yorkshire Post*, 22.2.1993 (Photocopy in Rock Garden Archive).

15. R. Desmond, *Dictionary of British and Irish Botanists and Horticulturalists* (Taylor & Francis and Natural History Museum, 1994).

16. K. Bradley-Hole, "Backhouse Nurseries, Yorkshire" in *Lost Gardens of England: from the Archives of Country Life* (Aurum Press, 2004), pp.180-183.

17. Obituary of James Backhouse, *Gardeners' Chronicle and Agricultural Gazette*, 13.9.1890, p.310.

18. W. Robinson, 1903, *op. cit.* frontispiece.

19. Royal Botanic Garden Edinburgh – Rock Garden. www.rbge.org.uk/the-gardens/edinburgh/garden-features/rock-garden (last accessed 1.2.2014)

20. W. Robinson, "Notes on Gardens No VI Backhouse's Nurseries, York (Third Notice)", *The Gardeners' Chronicle and Agricultural Gazette*, 2.4.1864, p.317.

21. W. Robinson, 1903, *op. cit.* p.30.

22. W. Robinson, 1864, *op. cit.* p.317.

23. H.N.H., 1875, *op. cit.* p.477.

24. J. McCulloch, *Initial Study into the Viability of Restoration of the Backhouse Rock Garden, West Bank Park, Holgate, York* (Unpublished report, Askham Bryan College, 1997), p.33.

25. "Messrs J. Backhouse and Son, York Nurseries", *York Illustrated*, 1894, p.23 (Photocopy in Rock Garden Archive).

26. M. Nieke, "West Bank Park and Holgate windmill", *Yorkshire Gardens Trust Newsletter*, Winter 2012, p.15.

27. R. Desmond, 1994, *op. cit.*

28. A. McConnell, "Crisp, Sir Frank, first baronet (1843 -1919)", *Oxford Dictionary of National Biography* (OUP, online edition, 2007). http://www.oxforddnb.com/view/article/49715 (last accessed 1.2.2014)

29. B. Elliott, 2011, *op. cit.*

30. W.A. Clark, *Alpine Plants – A practical method for growing the rarer and more difficult alpine flowers* (Upcott Gill, 1901).

31. *Ibid.* p.v.

32. P. Davis, "Backhouse family (per.c.1770 -1945)", *Oxford Dictionary of National Biography* (OUP, online edition, 2007). http://www.oxforddnb.com/view/article/56500/61919?docPos=3 (last accessed 1.2.2014)

33. "Agriculture and Botany – Important educational scheme at York", *Yorkshire Evening Post*, 18.12.1902, p.3.

34. E.H. Jenkins, *Rock Gardens and Alpine Plants* (W.H. & L. Collingridge, 1911) p.16.

35. *York Illustrated* article, 1894, *op. cit.* p.24.

36. James Backhouse and Son Ltd, *Alpine plants, hardy perennials and florists' flowers*, 1898 Catalogue, p.2.

37. N. Shulman, 2002, *op. cit.*

38. R. Farrer, *The Rock Garden* (T. Nelson and Son Ltd, 1912), pp. 8-9.

39. *Ibid.* p.12.

40. W. R. Mitchell, *Reginald Farrer: at home in the Yorkshire Dales* (Castleberg, 2002).

41. T. Waltham, *The Yorkshire Dales: landscape and geology* (The Crowood Press, 2007).

42. R. Farrer, 1912, *op. cit.* p.7.

Chapter Three

43. S. Moorhouse, "Anatomy of the Yorkshire Dales: decoding the medieval landscape" in T. Manby, S. Moorhouse and P. Ottaway (eds.), *The Archaeology of Yorkshire* (YAS, 2003), pp.293-362.

44. B. Harrison and B. Hutton, "The Western Uplands - the Northern Dales" in *Vernacular Houses in North Yorkshire and Cleveland* (John Donald Publishing Ltd, 1984), pp.216-220.

45. R. Kain and H. Prince, *Tithe Surveys for Historians* (Phillimore, 2000).

46. *Apportionment of the Rent-charge in lieu of Tithes in the township of Aysgarth in the county of York*, 1843, NYCRO T(PC/AYS).

47. *Plan of the township of Aysgarth*, 1843, NYCRO T(PC/AYS).

48. Last Will and Testament of Francis Sayer, 12.12.1871 (Photocopy in Rock Garden Archive).

49. D. Hey, "Census returns" in *The Oxford Companion to Family and Local History*, 2nd Edition (Oxford University Press, 2010), pp.309-312.

50. M. Hartley and J. Ingilby, *Life and Tradition in the Yorkshire Dales* (originally published 1968, this edition, Smith Settle Ltd, 1997).

51. E. Bogg, *Beautiful Wensleydale* (James Miles and Edmund Bogg, 1925), p.177.

52. *Aysgarth Union Valuation*, 1872, NYCRO DC/AYS.

53. E. Dennison, "Woodhall rabbit warren, Carperby" in R. White and P. Wilson (eds.), *Archaeology and Historic Landscapes of the Yorkshire Dales* (YAS, 2004), pp. 137-144.

54. M. Hartley and J. Ingilby, *A Dales Heritage* (Dalesman Books, 1984), p.108.

Chapter Four

55. H. Speight, *Romantic Richmondshire* (Elliot Stock, 1897), p.444.

56. J. Hatcher, *Richmondshire Architecture* (C.J. Hatcher, 1990).

57. James Backhouse and Son Ltd, *Alpine and herbaceous plants*, 1911 Catalogue, endpiece.

58. B. Elliott, 2011, *op. cit.* p.41, quoting from anonymous articles in *The Garden*, 1923.

59. W.A. Clark, *Alpine Plants – A practical manual for their culture*, 2nd Edition (Upcott Gill, 1907).

60. "Alpine plants and their culture - Interesting work by a York expert - Wonderful alpine and Japanese water gardens", *The Yorkshire Herald*, February 1907 (Photocopy in Rock Garden Archive).

61. *Ibid.*

62. W.A. Clark, 1907, *op. cit.* frontispiece.

63. Postcard of Aysgarth, postmarked York, August 3rd 1906 (Personal collection of Denny Gibson).

64. H.N.H., 1875, *op. cit.* p.478.

65. Capstone Consulting Engineers, *Aysgarth Edwardian Rock Garden, North Yorkshire, Structural Engineering Appraisal.* (Unpublished report, 2002), p.3.

66. Ancient Society of York Florists. http://www.ancientsocietyofyorkflorists.co.uk/History.htm (last accessed 1.2.2014)

67. James Backhouse and Son Ltd, *Alpine and herbaceous plants*, 1911 Catalogue, frontispiece.

68. R.A. Malby, *The Story of my Rock Garden*, 3rd Edition (Headley Brothers, 1913).

Chapter Five

69. R. Blakesley, *The Arts and Crafts Movement* (Phaidon Press Ltd, 2006).

70. *St Andrew's Church Aysgarth – A visitors' guide*, 2009, p.11.

71. Ralph Hedley. http://en.wikipedia.org/wiki/Ralph_Hedley (last accessed 1.2.2014)

72. 1st Codicil to Last Will and Testament of Francis Sayer Graham, 21.4.1925 (Photocopy in Rock Garden Archive).

73. D. Webster, *Kiplin Hall and the Arts and Crafts Movement* (Kiplin Hall leaflet, 2007).

74. Last Will and Testament of Francis Sayer Graham, 6.3.1917 (Photocopy in Rock Garden Archive).

75. 1st Codicil of F.S Graham, 1925, *op. cit.*

76. Last Will and Testament of Mary Elizabeth Graham, 8.5.1911 (Typewritten transcript in Rock Garden Archive).

77. 2nd Codicil to Last Will and Testament of Francis Sayer Graham, 2.5.1931 (Photocopy in Rock Garden Archive).

78. 6th Codicil to Last Will and Testament of Francis Sayer Graham, 26.5.1941 (Photocopy in Rock Garden Archive).

79. Last Will and Testament of F. S. Graham, 1917, *op. cit.*

80. "Public Service to Wensleydale", Unknown newspaper obituary, July 1946 (Photocopy in Rock Garden Archive).

81. A. Mee, *The King's England: Yorkshire, North Riding* (Hodder and Stoughton, 1941), p.26.

82. Unknown newspaper obituary, July 1946, *op. cit.*

83. 1st Codicil of F.S. Graham, 1925, *op. cit.*

84. Unknown newspaper obituary, July 1946, *op. cit.*

85. J. Pemberton, *Will Pickles of Wensleydale: the life of a country doctor* (Country Book Club, 1970).

86. W. Pickles, *Epidemiology in Country Practice* (RCGP, 1984, First published 1939).

87. *Heather Cottage, Aysgarth, Yorks. Catalogue of the antique and modern furniture etc to be sold by auction, 18th and 19th June, 1947*, J.W. Arnett, Darlington (Photocopy in Rock Garden Archive).

88. Unknown newspaper obituary, July 1946, *op. cit.*

89. F.S. Graham, "Swallows and House Martins in Wensleydale", Letter to the Editor of *The Northern Echo*, 28.11.1938 (Photocopy in Rock Garden Archive).

Chapter Six

90. B.A. Bailey, "Isham, Sir Charles Edmund, tenth baronet (1819-1903)", Oxford Dictionary of National Biography (OUP, online edition, 2007). http://www.oxforddnb.com/view/article/66117 (last accessed 1.2.2014)

91. *RHS Chelsea Centenary: 100 years of the RHS Chelsea Flower Show*, Supplement to *The Garden*, May, 2013.

92. M. Nieke, 2012, *op. cit.*

93. B. Elliott, 2011, *op. cit.*

94. J. McCulloch, 1997, *op. cit.*

95. "Many disappointed at York Nurseries sale", Unknown newspaper report, 1.12.1955 (Photocopy in Rock Garden Archive).

96. J. McCulloch, 1997, *op. cit.*

97. Untitled report, *Manchester Courier and Lancashire Advertiser*, 20.9.1905, p.7.

98. W.A. Clark, 1907, *op. cit.* frontispiece.

99. "York man's gift to Princess Mary", *Yorkshire Herald*, 1922 (stuck into endpapers of 1901 edition of W.A. Clark, *Alpine Plants*).

100. Obituary of Mr William Angus Clark, *Yorkshire Gazette*, 10.2.1950.

Chapter Seven

101. J. Makin, *Aysgarth Rock Garden – Report and Management Plan* (Unpublished report, 2002).

102. Capstone Consulting Engineers, 2002, *op. cit.*

Afterword

103. D.E. Schaper, *The Art of Spiritual Rock Gardening* (Hidden Spring, 2001), front flap.